Contents

Handy Cookery Charts · *page* 6

How to Use this Book · 7

INTRODUCTION · 9
The medical background

GUIDELINES ON COOKING AND MENU PLANNING · · · · · · 17
Putting a cholesterol-lowering diet into practice

HEALTHY MENUS FOR EVERY DAY · · · · · · · · · · · · · · 20
Main and lighter family meals, including breakfasts

MENUS FOR HEALTHY ENTERTAINING · · · · · · · · · · · · 30
Imaginative, well-planned menus for every occasion

RECIPE SECTION · 57
From soups and starters through to snacks, sauces and
home baking

USEFUL TABLES · 117
Saturated fat and cholesterol chart, plus calorie counts

INDEX · 124

Handy Cookery Charts

CONVERSION TO METRIC MEASUREMENTS

The metric measures in this book are based on a 25 g unit instead of the ounce (28·35 g). Slight adjustments to this basic conversion standard were necessary in some recipes to achieve satisfactory cooking results.

If you want to convert your own recipes from imperial to metric, we suggest you use the same 25 g unit, and use 600 ml in place of 1 pint, with the British Standard 5-ml and 15-ml spoons replacing the old variable teaspoons and tablespoons; these adaptations will sometimes give a slightly smaller recipe quantity and may require a shorter cooking time.

Note Sets of British Standard metric measuring spoons are available in the following sizes – 2·5 ml, 5 ml, 10 ml and 15 ml.

When measuring milk it is more convenient to the the exact conversion of 568 ml (1 pint).

For more general reference, the following tables will be helpful.

METRIC CONVERSION SCALE

Liquid			**Solid**		
Imperial	*Exact conversion*	*Recommended ml*	*Imperial*	*Exact conversion*	*Recommended g*
¼ pint	142 ml	150 ml	1 oz	28·35 g	25 g
½ pint	284 ml	300 ml	2 oz	56·7 g	50 g
1 pint	568 ml	600 ml	4 oz	113·4 g	100 g
1½ pints	851 ml	900 ml	8 oz	226·8 g	225 g
1¾ pints	992 ml	1 litre	12 oz	340·2 g	325 g
			14 oz	397·0 g	400 g
For quantities of 1¾ pints and over, litres and fractions of a litre have been used.			16 oz (1 lb)	453·6 g	450 g
			1 kilogram (kg) equals 2·2 lb		

Note Follow either the metric or the imperial measures in the recipes as they are not interchangeable.

OVEN TEMPERATURE CHART

°C	°F	*Gas mark*
120	225	¼
130	250	½
140	275	1
150	300	2
170	325	3
180	350	4
190	375	5
200	400	6
220	425	7
230	450	8
240	475	9

GOOD HOUSEKEEPING
Healthy Eating, Healthy Heart

GOOD HOUSEKEEPING
Healthy Eating, Healthy Heart

by
Good Housekeeping Institute

EBURY PRESS
LONDON

Published by Ebury Press
National Magazine House
72 Broadwick Street
London W1V 2BP

First impression 1979

ISBN 0 85223 151 2

Designer Derek Morrison
Line drawings by Vanessa Luff
Colour photography by Roger Tuff

Cover photograph shows
Chicken in plum sauce
(*page 84*)

China and glass for the
colour photographs facing pages 32 and 33,
and for the cover photograph, was supplied by
the General Trading Company Limited,
144 Sloane Street, London SW1X 9BL.

Filmset and printed in Great Britain by
BAS Printers Limited, Over Wallop, Hampshire
and bound by
William Brendon and Son Limited, Tiptree, Essex

How to Use this Book

QUANTITIES

Recipes give 4 servings, unless otherwise specified.

CHOLESTEROL RATINGS

We have used symbols to grade each recipe according to its cholesterol content, as follows:

○ Nil to low cholesterol content – these are dishes which can be freely included in the diet

◐ Low to medium cholesterol content – do not eat these dishes too often

● Medium to high cholesterol content – have these dishes only on special occasions or not at all if your diet is a very strict one

CALORIE COUNTING

We have given calories for 1 serving of every recipe, unless otherwise indicated.

The first figure gives calories and applies to the imperial version of the recipe: the second figure (in brackets) gives joules and applies to the metric version.

USING THE RIGHT FAT

To be sure of buying a fat which is suitable for a cholesterol-lowering diet look on the label and check that, like Flora margarine, it says 'high in polyunsaturates'.

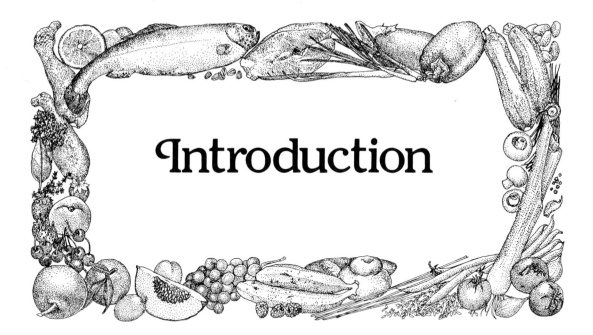

Introduction

It is now 25 years since it was first suggested that coronary heart disease (CHD) is linked with the amount of fat in the diet. Since then there has been a vast amount of research on this topic – and on CHD in general. In recent years the evidence has been considered at length by at least 21 different expert committees in a number of countries, and they have all made specific dietary recommendations for the prevention of CHD. These recommendations predominantly concern the amount and type of fat in our diets. In the following pages we try to answer a number of important questions about the disease and the role diet may play in preventing it.

What is CHD?

The heart is a powerful muscular pump and, like all muscles, it is well supplied with blood by the coronary arteries and their branches. As we get older these arteries harden because there is a build up of a fatty porridge-like scarring on the inside of the artery walls. This disorder, known as atherosclerosis, narrows the channel of the artery and limits the flow of blood. Often this causes few, if any, problems but it can lead to angina or a heart attack (coronary thrombosis).

A person with angina develops pain in the chest during activity. This is due to the abnormality in the coronary artery which prevents the heart muscle getting the extra blood it needs during exercise. At rest there is no pain, for although the coronary artery is obstructed, the channel is still large enough to allow sufficient blood through. In a heart attack, however, the blood flow through a narrowed coronary artery stops completely. When this happens, part of the heart muscle stops functioning and the victim feels cold and sweaty and complains of severe chest pain. Heart attacks can occur suddenly, out of the blue, but often the attack can be preceded by short bouts of chest pain or by increasingly severe angina.

Who is at risk?

The risk of developing CHD has risen alarmingly over the past fifty years. At a conservative estimate about one in every three or four men in their late 50s or early 60s have CHD to some extent or another. But

CHD is not restricted to this age group. Indeed, one of the major concerns is the increasing tendency for CHD to develop in younger men. Neither are women immune, although they tend not to develop CHD until after the menopause. More disturbing still is the fact that atherosclerosis, the condition which leads to CHD, seems already to be increasingly well established in adolescence and early adulthood.

What can be done about CHD?

Although a great deal can be done to relieve or treat CHD, with drugs or, in some cases, surgery, it is not yet possible to cure it. And since it is always more sensible to prevent illness, much of the research has been directed towards discovering the cause of this condition and developing effective methods of prevention.

However, in spite of all the research it has not been possible to show that CHD is due to one unique cause – as, for example, the cause of measles is known to be the measles virus. A large number of different factors are associated with CHD and – what is more important – they appear to put an individual affected by these factors at particular risk. They are often called 'risk' factors.

Risk factors can be constitutional or environmental. For example, an individual's chances of having a heart attack depends on constitutional factors such as his sex, age, blood pressure, body weight and blood cholesterol level. (Cholesterol is a fatty substance present in all human tissue and is discussed in detail on page 12.) Conditions such as diabetes, certain hormone disorders, abnormalities in blood clotting mechanisms or antibody reactions also influence the degree of risk – and there may be others which have not yet been identified. Environmental factors are also important. These include smoking, physical inactivity, the diet, the stress of modern life and a number of other social factors. Personality may also be involved –

for example, a person's level of tension and anxiety. However, the three major risk factors are high blood cholesterol, heavy smoking and high blood pressure.

Although there is an association between the above risk factors and CHD this association does not necessarily imply that they are the cause of the condition. The fact that a particular individual has one or other of the risk factors does not mean that he will inevitably become a victim of a heart attack – it only implies that he runs a higher risk. For example, it is true that on average more heavy cigarette smokers die from CHD than non-smokers. But many know from their own experience of non-smokers who have had heart attacks, and of men who have smoked heavily for many years without developing even a hint of CHD.

Another fact to remember is that risk factors are themselves associated one with another. The overweight person tends to take little exercise, cigarette smokers tend to smoke more when under stress or pressure, and so on. But perhaps more importantly, risk factors also interact with or reinforce one another. An individual who smokes heavily, has high blood pressure and a high blood cholesterol level has a far higher risk of developing CHD than a person with only one of these risk factors. The implication of this is that all risk factors must be modified if CHD is to be successfully prevented. Modifying one – for example, by giving up smoking – will not make up for your over-indulgence in dietary fat or your high blood pressure, though it will go some way towards reducing the risk.

*   *   *

Even though the aim of this book is to help you to reduce the level of cholesterol in the blood by eating a cholesterol-lowering diet, it might be interesting to have a brief look at some of the other risk factors – smoking, high blood pressure, physical inactivity and stress.

Cigarette smoking has been shown conclusively to increase the risk of coronary thrombosis and the rate at which atherosclerosis develops. Smoking 20 cigarettes per day increases the risk three-fold compared with the non-smoker, though the risk is lower in cigar and pipe smokers. So giving up reduces the risk considerably.

High blood pressure is also associated with an increased risk of CHD, probably because it not only damages the wall of the artery but also accelerates atherosclerosis. Treatment for high blood pressure reduces a major risk factor.

Physical inactivity The first evidence that physical activity is related to CHD came from studies of men in different occupations. It was found that physically active workers (such as bus conductors) suffered less disease than people doing sedentary work (the bus drivers). Further studies have tended to confirm this, and show that regular vigorous exercise taken at weekends also gives some measure of protection. On the whole, however, it is best to take a little exercise every day, and if you decide to start doing this, begin gradually or seek medical advice.

Stress and personality These factors are widely held to be important in the development of CHD. However, the scientific evidence to support this is frequently questioned by doctors. Probably it is true to say that they contribute in some way, but they are not a major factor. Personality, of course, can be rather difficult to change.

Overweight and other effects of diet

The expert committees have recommended that we limit our total calorie intake so that we do not become overweight. The wisest way of doing this is to restrict the intake of sugar, sugary foods and alcohol which are all high calorie foods. Trace metals such as zinc and copper, vitamins and high blood levels of other fatty substances have also been suggested as risk factors.

There is, on the other hand, some evidence that dietary fibre exerts a protective effect against CHD. Dietary fibre is what adds bulk or roughage to our diets and its role in preventing constipation is well known. It comes primarily from the cell wall of plants so it is present in fruits, vegetables and seeds such as wheat, oats and barley. In underdeveloped countries the intake of dietary fibre is particularly high as about 75% of the calorie intake consists of unrefined or only partially refined plant foods. In the west, plant foods account for only about 30% of the calorie intake, and they are mostly highly refined products such as white sugar or white flour. The suggestion is that an over-refined diet could be adding to the effect of a high cholesterol diet in contributing to CHD mortality. It is borne out by studies which show that even in affluent countries CHD tends to be less common among those who eat high-fibre diets.

Plant fibres reduce blood cholesterol by absorbing the waste products produced by the liver when it metabolises cholesterol. This seems to stimulate the liver into metabolising more and more cholesterol, and

as a result the blood cholesterol level falls. Recent research shows that some plant fibres are more effective than others. For example, rolled oats seem to have a better lowering effect than wheat and pectin, lignin and other plant gums better than cellulose or the fibrous residue of sugar.

Various foods we eat, then, exert good or bad influences, but the main topic of interest as far as the diet is concerned is the association between cholesterol and CHD.

What is cholesterol?

Cholesterol is a fatty substance which is present in all human tissue, including blood. It performs essential functions in the body – but it also contributes to atherosclerosis since it is an integral part of the fatty porridge-like thickening inside the affected arteries. Cholesterol either comes directly from cholesterol rich foods in the diet or is manufactured by the body, mainly from foods rich in saturated fats. All foods of animal origin, such as meat, contain cholesterol, and egg yolks, offal, butter and cream are particularly high. Saturated fats are also, generally speaking, animal fats such as lard, suet, mutton fat, butter and hard cheese, though the hard vegetable fats, hard margarine for example, are also included in this category. They are the hard fats which are solid at room temperature. Plants contain no cholesterol, so fruits, vegetables and vegetable oils are cholesterol free.

How is cholesterol linked with CHD?

It has been known for many years that countries whose populations have, on average, lower blood cholesterol levels than those found in affluent western communities also have a lower death rate resulting from CHD. This was initially demonstrated in a study involving 7 countries – Finland, Greece, Holland, Italy, Japan, America and Yugoslavia – just over 25 years ago. This showed, for example, that the average blood cholesterol level of a man living in a small Japanese fishing village was about half that of a man living in the rural areas of Finland – and the difference in the number of CHD deaths was equally dramatic. The death rate in Japan was the lowest among the seven countries and Finland's the highest – ten times that of Japan.

Since then, the relationship between high blood cholesterol and high CHD mortality has been reaffirmed in over 20 studies. It has also been shown that there is a definite stepwise relationship between the two, i.e. the higher the blood cholesterol level, the higher the risk of developing CHD. In the original 7 countries studied, the 5 other countries took intermediate positions between the Japanese low and Finnish high CHD mortality rates, and the order varied in accordance with the corresponding blood cholesterol levels.

This stepwise relationship between blood cholesterol level and risk of developing CHD holds good not only for communities as a whole but also for groups of men within a community. Several large studies, again in many countries, have confirmed this and have allowed doctors to assess the probability of the risk more accurately. For example, results of a study in Framingham, Massachusetts, show that the probability of a man aged 40 to 59 developing CHD within 10 years is directly related to his blood cholesterol level. A 40 year old man with a blood cholesterol level over 280 mg per 100 ml of blood (230 mg per 100 ml can be regarded as normal) is four times as likely to have a heart attack as one with a level below about 200 mg per 100 ml. And people with rare inherited conditions causing exceptionally high blood cholesterol levels are quite likely to experience their first symptoms of CHD during adolescence.

What is the link between diet, cholesterol and CHD?

The Seven Countries study referred to earlier showed that the Japanese fishermen had, on average, a much lower blood cholesterol level than the Finns. The study also showed another remarkable difference – in the diet. The Japanese diet was low in cholesterol-forming saturated fats and cholesterol, whereas the Finnish diet contained large amounts. This suggests that a diet high in saturated fats and cholesterol leads to high blood cholesterol levels which are in turn associated with a higher risk of developing CHD. Further comparisons of national dietary intakes, blood cholesterol levels and CHD mortality confirmed this association. For example, CHD is low in underdeveloped countries where the intake of saturated fats and cholesterol is low, but has reached almost epidemic proportions in the affluent western countries where the intake of these foodstuffs is particularly high. It has been observed that people emigrating from a low to high risk country have an increasing tendency to develop CHD as they adopt the host country's dietary habits.

Does a change in diet alter cholesterol levels?

The next step was to determine whether blood cholesterol levels could be influenced by dietary changes. Investigations over the past 20 years have shown that this is reasonably easy to do. An increase in saturated fats – hard vegetable fats and those of animal origin such as lard, suet, mutton fat, butter and cheese – and in cholesterol rich foods, is followed by an increase in blood cholesterol in most individuals. This is not surprising, realising as we do that the body makes most of its cholesterol from dietary saturated fats. Conversely, blood cholesterol levels can be reduced by reducing the amount of saturated fat and cholesterol in the diet. This has been demonstrated not only in adults but also in adolescents and children and the cholesterol lowering effect is maintained as long as the dietary restrictions are heeded. These notable findings are the basis of the dietary prevention of CHD.

The cholesterol theory gains further support from studies on groups of individuals such as vegetarians and Seventh Day Adventists. CHD mortality amongst male Seventh Day Adventists is approximately 40% less than the general population. This has been attributed, at least in part, to their lower consumption of meat and animal fats. Vegetarians also have a much lower risk of developing CHD, and their blood cholesterol levels are again usually considerably below the national average. This particular benefit of a vegetarian diet shows itself even in young people – the blood cholesterol levels of vegetarian adolescents are significantly lower than those of adolescents eating a normal meat and animal products diet.

The role of polyunsaturated fats

Reducing the amount of saturated fats and cholesterol in the diet is not the only effective way of lowering blood cholesterol. Polyunsaturated fats also play an important part, and it has been shown many times that when they are *added* to the diet they reduce the blood cholesterol level appreciably. This special role has been recognised for almost thirty years.

The polyunsaturated fats are the very

soft or oily fats, mostly of vegetable origin, such as corn, sunflower seed and soya bean oil. The extent of the drop in blood cholesterol they produce is roughly related to the ratio of polyunsaturated to saturated fats in the diet. In this respect, lowering the amount of the three commonest saturated fatty acids does have a much greater effect – twice the effect in fact – than adding extra polyunsaturated fats to the diet. Polyunsaturated fats are nevertheless very useful, and their cholesterol lowering effect has been observed in all age groups, including adolescents.

But not only do polyunsaturated fats have an acknowledged reducing effect on blood cholesterol; they also have another important property. Some polyunsaturated fats, in particular sunflower seed oil, corn oil and the margarines made predominantly from these oils, have a high linoleic acid content. As well as being a vital nutrient, this acid is an essential ingredient of a newly discovered class of hormones called the prostaglandins. These have a variety of physiological effects, including the important ability to reduce platelet stickiness. The platelets are blood cells whose main task is to stick together to form a clot when this is necessary. If the platelets become abnormally sticky there is a risk that they might form clots, for example, on an atherosclerotic area in one of the coronary arteries. Such a clot, or thrombus, would obstruct the flow of blood to the heart muscle and lead to a heart attack (coronary thrombosis).

In other words, polyunsaturated fats could act in at least two separate ways to reduce the risk of CHD – firstly by reducing blood cholesterol levels and secondly by helping in the manufacture of the prostaglandins which prevent the platelets becoming abnormally sticky.

What is a cholesterol-lowering diet?

Blood cholesterol levels can be reduced by changing the amount and type of fat in our diet. These changes are a lot less drastic than they sound and the cholesterol-lowering diet is an interesting and varied one which can be easily adapted to accommodate most food preferences. There are two basic points to remember.

First, it is necessary to *reduce* the total amount of fat, particularly saturated fat and cholesterol, in your normal diet. In practical terms this means eating less saturated (animal) fat and other animal products which are rich in cholesterol. For example, you should avoid suet, lard, dripping, white cooking fat and hard margarine as well as cutting off all visible fat from meat before eating it. It is also wise to cut down on dairy produce, especially cream, full fat cheese and butter, and foods such as shop bought cakes and biscuits which are often prepared from saturated fats. Chicken, veal and fish should be eaten in preference to pork, lamb and beef. Foods which are naturally rich in cholesterol should also be restricted. These include egg yolks, offal and cream, butter and full fat cheese. Substitute low fat yogurt, cottage cheese and skimmed milk for dairy produce and eat as much as you like of fruit, vegetables and cereals.

Second, as well as reducing the intake of saturated fat and cholesterol, it is necessary to *increase* the intake of polyunsaturated fats – mostly the vegetable oils – since these also help to lower the blood cholesterol level. In practical terms this means substituting polyunsaturated margarine for butter, and using corn, soya or sunflower oil instead of hard fats. This may mean some changes in your cooking methods initially, but you soon get used to it and the finished dishes not only look similar but taste the same, or even better.

These may be all the dietary guidelines you are given if you have been advised to go on a cholesterol-lowering diet. You might, quite understandably, be uncertain exactly how to apply them and how to integrate them into a pattern of sensible eating for the

whole family. The following chapters are full of detailed information on the practical aspects of the diet. You will find helpful advice on choosing and planning family menus as well as recipes for meals to cook for special occasions.

How effective is a cholesterol-lowering diet?

The cholesterol-lowering properties of diets low in saturated fats and cholesterol and high in polyunsaturated fats are not disputed. Studies which have evaluated the effectiveness of the diet have basically been of two types. The first type are the primary preventive trials where the aim is to prevent CHD appearing in healthy individuals, and the second type are the secondary preventive trials where the aim is to prevent further heart attacks in men who have already succumbed to CHD.

The major findings in both types of study are that blood cholesterol levels can be reduced, and that the lower levels can be maintained as long as the individual stays on the diet. These trials have also proved that the diet is acceptable, even in cultures where it represents a significant change from the normal diet.

Taken as a whole, the long term benefit of such a diet has not been proven beyond a doubt, although the evidence is clearly very suggestive. There is a handful of reports indicating that such a diet has actually produced an improvement in the atherosclerosis affecting some arteries, though it is probably too early to be sure of this yet.

On a national scale, there is a suggestion that the rise in CHD mortality is beginning to slow down. This has been observed in America and Australia and some experts believe it reflects increasing public awareness of dangers of over-eating and smoking. In Britain, the overall rise in CHD mortality has not slowed down, although there are signs that it might do so and already CHD mortality is rising less sharply amongst groups of people who have altered their eating and smoking habits. Efforts to obtain more definite proof continue in many countries. There is, for example, a major preventive trial in progress in Finland, where the CHD mortality is particularly high.

The experts' conclusions

In the past decade at least 21 expert committees have considered the vast amount of experimental, statistical and medical evidence on CHD and diet and all have made recommendations about the fat in our diets. However, in order to obtain the most benefit from their advice we must realise that they are not 'blanket' recommendations for every individual. There are different groups within the community and the advice for each group varies in degree if not necessarily in type.

The high risk group

The group most in need of dietary changes are those who have abnormally high blood levels of cholesterol. In these cases the experts advise a strict diet. Saturated fat and cholesterol intake must be restricted, and polyunsaturated fat intake increased.

Often the diet may have to be modified in other ways – by reducing the carbohydrate content for example – and special fat lowering drugs may also be necessary. These kinds of abnormalities are rare and do not affect many people.

For the individual who has a higher than average blood cholesterol level the expert committees also recommend restriction of saturated fats and cholesterol and substitution of polyunsaturated fats. But they make the point that any other risk factor, such as smoking, high blood pressure or physical inactivity, must also be modified to reduce the risk of CHD.

Other people
The vast majority of people are not in the high-risk group, but a significant number may certainly have higher than average blood cholesterol levels. As it is impractical to organise the widespread screening necessary to discover the exact blood cholesterol level of every single person, the experts agree that it is wise for everyone, however healthy he feels, to try to cut down on saturated fats.

At present well over 40% of our intake of calories is as fat, and most of this is as saturated fat. The experts agree that this should drop at least to about 35%, though they are not totally agreed that it is necessary for everyone to increase their intake of polyunsaturated fats. Of the 19 committees who made specific recommendations for the healthy majority of people, 17, including that of the Royal College of Physicians in conjunction with the British Cardiac Society, suggested that polyunsaturates should be increased, while 2, one of which was the group organised by the Department of Health and Social Security, did not think such an increase was necessary.

Our children
Children who have abnormally high blood cholesterol levels will need to follow a strict cholesterol-lowering diet throughout life, and the diet is also advisable for children who are known to have conditions which put them at particular risk of developing CHD. Children in these two special groups are generally given the correct dietary advice for their specific needs by their own doctors. Other children, the healthy majority, will benefit as much as their parents from eating a cholesterol-lowering diet. There are many advantages. The whole family can eat the same meals, meaning that separate menus need not be planned for one or two individuals; the diet is nutritionally well balanced and will start children on a lifetime of good eating habits; and although it is not designed as a slimming diet, it does help to prevent people from gaining weight. It might even help prevent dental caries as many of the between meal snacks which make this problem worse would be banned because of their saturated fat and cholesterol content.

But the major reason for encouraging healthy children to eat a cholesterol-lowering diet would be to reduce the risk of their developing CHD. It is of course important that they should also be encouraged to take regular vigorous exercise and to avoid smoking, but atherosclerosis is known to begin in adolescence and it is reasonable to suppose that a cholesterol-lowering diet might at least slow down its development and so reduce the CHD risk.

The experts' conclusions, therefore, lead us to believe that there is no group of people which would not benefit from following a cholesterol-lowering diet. Practical advice on how to put their recommendations into practice is given in the next chapter, 'Guidelines on cooking and menu planning'.

DR SUSAN GARTH
Medical Adviser to Good Housekeeping

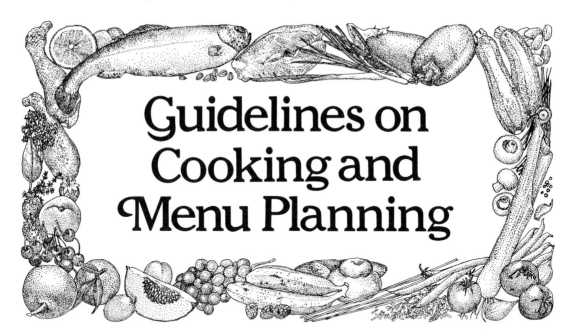

Guidelines on Cooking and Menu Planning

It is all very well being told to cut down on saturated fats and rich sources of cholesterol, but what does this mean in practical terms? General recommendations are helpful, but it is much simpler to look in a fair amount of detail at what you can and cannot eat.

How to cut down on saturated fats

(a) Restrict or eliminate fats such as butter, hard margarine, suet, lard, dripping and white cooking fats. Avoid oil or soft margarines not clearly marked as being 'high in polyunsaturated fats'.

(b) Don't eat obviously fatty meat. Choose lean cuts only, and before you cook them use a sharp knife to trim off all visible fat. Eat less lamb and beef, and pork only very occasionally. Grill rather than fry meat so that fat can easily be discarded.

(c) Cut down on all dairy produce, particularly creams – double, single and soured – and full fat cheeses – Cheddar, Cheshire, Stilton, cream cheeses and Danish Blue.

(d) Avoid ready made dishes as these often contain hidden eggs, cream and butter. Cakes, biscuits, pastry, ice cream, mayonnaise, sauces and soups are a few of the main ones to look out for. Sorbets and water based ices are a pleasant alternative to ice cream.

How to avoid rich sources of cholesterol

(a) Limit the number of eggs you eat. For a strict diet the recommended limit is three per week. Remember the hidden eggs in prepared foods – these must be counted in your weekly allowance.

(b) On a very strict diet cut out the offal meats altogether. Even on a less strict diet, liver, heart and kidney should be rationed and sweetbreads and brains should be avoided whenever possible.

(c) Some shellfish is high in cholesterol. Avoid shrimps, prawns and roe, remembering that roe is one of the main ingredients of the popular fish pâté, Taramasalata.

(d) As well as being rich in saturated fats, butter, cream and full fat cheese are also high in cholesterol, which makes it doubly important to replace them with the low fat alternatives discussed on page 18.

Every recipe in this book has been created with a low cholesterol diet in mind, but it is obvious that some are going to be lower in

17

cholesterol than others. To help you plan your diet we have devised a system of symbols and used them to grade each recipe according to its cholesterol content, as follows:

○ Nil to low cholesterol content – these dishes may be included freely in the diet.

◑ Low to medium cholesterol content – these should only be eaten occasionally.

● Medium to high cholesterol content – eat these dishes only on special occasions, or not at all if you are on a very strict diet.

Consult the chart on pages 117–118 for the cholesterol and saturated fat content of a variety of popular foods. Remember that fruit and vegetables are cholesterol free and include as many as you can eat.

The main culprits, then, are meat, high fat dairy produce, egg yolks, hard margarine, hard cooking fats, cakes and pastries. Now that we have discussed the foods you ought to cut down on, let's look at the healthier alternatives. There is nothing 'cranky' about them – in fact some of them may already be amongst your favourite foods.

Meat and fish you can eat

From the chart on page 117, giving saturated fat and cholesterol ratings, it is obvious that more meals should be planned around poultry, rabbit and veal. Lamb and beef may be included occasionally but fatty cuts of pork should really be avoided altogether.

Choose the leanest cuts of any meat and use a sharp knife to trim off visible fat before cooking. Remove the skin from poultry where possible. Cook casseroles and stews the day before you want to eat them; once they have cooled the surface layer of animal fat can easily be removed. Dishes based on minced meats such as beef or veal should be made from meat bought in one lean piece, trimmed of all visible fat and minced at home. Meat bought ready minced from the

butcher tends to be rather fatty but if you do have to use it, it helps to dry fry it in a non-stick pan, discarding the fat which melts out before adding the mince to the dish.

White fish is an excellent choice and should play a major part in your cholesterol-lowering diet. It is as rich in protein as it is low in cholesterol and doesn't always have to be covered in batter and deep fat fried. The economical varieties can be made into delicious family meals, while the more expensive sole, turbot and halibut, cooked in interesting ways, are ideal for the most sophisticated dinner party. A fish brick, for example, is an excellent way of combining the delicate flavours of fish and fresh herbs or spices.

Dairy produce you can eat

It is surprisingly easy to live without milk, cream and full fat cheeses. Skimmed milk may always be substituted for whole milk and can either be bought as separated milk from your milkman or reconstituted from skimmed milk powder. Keep a jug, covered, in the refrigerator, ready for use in cooking and drinks. For milk with a little more 'body', there is a recipe for polyunsaturated filled milk on page 116. Natural low fat yogurt, cottage cheese and Edam cheese, made from partially skimmed milk, are ideal substitutes for cream, soured cream and full fat cheeses in many of the classic recipes. A spoonful or two of yogurt gives extra lift to sauces and casseroles.

Cholesterol-lowering diet for the overweight

A cholesterol-lowering diet is certainly a step on the way to losing some weight but it is not in itself a weight reducing diet. By cutting down on rich, fatty foods you certainly ought, if you are at all overweight, to lose a few surplus pounds, but if you have a figure problem as well as a heart problem it is important to remember that fats are not the only things that are fattening; a cholesterol-lowering diet doesn't automatically mean a low calorie one. Peanuts are a good example – low in cholesterol but very high in calories.

If you definitely need to lose weight, try to do it gradually by cutting out sugar, preserves, cakes, pastries, biscuits and alcohol. A more rapid weight loss can be achieved by a combination of increased physical activity and a calorie controlled diet.

In order to help you lose weight on a low cholesterol diet, **we have given the calorie count of one serving of every recipe (i.e. one quarter of the recipe except where otherwise indicated).** The first figure is in calories and applies to the imperial version of the recipe; the second figure (in brackets) is in joules and applies to the metric version. Obviously it will make sense to use more of the lower calorie recipes and fewer of the more fattening ones, trying to keep the daily count to about 6,270 kj or 1,500 kcals. To help you keep track of calories for basic foods and an even wider variety of recipes, use the charts on pages 119–123. It is not the difficult juggling act you may imagine to reduce weight and cholesterol intake at the same time.

Cooking the polyunsaturated way

Having chosen the most suitable foods, it is extremely important to cook them in the correct way. All the good will be undone if you fry your chicken or white fish in a large amount of butter, lard or dripping. Where possible, it is better not to fry at all, choosing cuts of meat and fish that can be grilled, roasted on a rack or spit roasted. This way, the saturated fat which melts out during cooking can easily be discarded.

When you do have to fry, you should use an oil or margarine which is high in polyunsaturated fats. Whereas frying white fish in lard turns an ideal choice of dish into a meal rich in cholesterol and saturated fats, cooking the same fish in a vegetable oil such as sunflower oil not only overcomes this problem but has the added advantage of providing some polyunsaturated fats which have, in their own right, a cholesterol-lowering effect. Remember to get the fat quite hot before starting to cook. This will prevent too much of it being absorbed by the food. Always drain fried foods thoroughly on kitchen paper towel.

When roasting meat, always stand it on a rack in the roasting tin and prick it all over to allow the fat to be released during cooking. Cover it with aluminium foil and roast in the usual way, but do not add saturated fats to the joint and do not baste during the cooking time. If you wish to serve gravy, do not make it with the fat from the joint but follow the recipe on page 115.

A high polyunsaturated margarine such as Flora is extremely versatile. It can be used successfully in home baking for cakes and pastries. If you make these yourself rather than buying them you will be quite certain that they contain no saturated fats and will know the exact number of eggs they contain for inclusion in your weekly allowance. A polyunsaturated margarine can be used for spreading, glazing vegetables and making sauces; margarine or oil, or a mixture of the two, should be used for shallow frying, greasing tins, and if necessary for basting and roasting; oil is ideal for deep frying, roasting and for making salad dressings.

So feel cheered by the thought that, provided it is cooked the cholesterol-lowering way, traditional roast beef and Yorkshire pudding need not be banished from your healthy heart diet.

Healthy Menus for Every Day

No 'healthy' member of the family need ever feel that he has to eat uninteresting meals because of someone else's cholesterol-lowering diet. One of our aims in this book has been to show what a wide variety of foods you *can* eat, and the essence of success is maintaining a balance.

Start with the main meal. You will probably want to include meat or fish, two of our main sources of protein, and we have already seen that some varieties are lower in cholesterol than others. Every recipe in this book has been given a cholesterol rating – 'low', 'medium' or 'high' – and it is sensible to plan as many 'low' meals as possible, based on poultry, white fish or veal, with a sprinkling of 'medium' lamb or beef-based meals to add variety. If you do have the odd 'high' rating main meal, compensate with a low cholesterol one the following day. The remaining meals of the day, breakfast and a light lunch or supper, should be 'low' or 'medium', and if you want to use recipes not included in this book you will be able to find out the cholesterol values of the ingredients by consulting the chart we have included at the end of the book.

A cholesterol-lowering diet is not the same thing as a slimming diet and we have included recipes for delicious desserts and puddings. Similarly, the flour and sugar in cakes and baking need only be avoided if on a strict slimming diet, so you can indulge in home baking as long as you remember to take any eggs and fats used from your weekly ration. What you do have to avoid are shop-bought cakes, pastries and biscuits, and things like ice cream and mayonnaise. You can never be certain what goes into them but it is more than likely that they will contain a high percentage of harmful saturated fats. Turn your attention towards things you can eat as often as you like – fruit and vegetables are full of vitamins and minerals and absolutely free of cholesterol.

The way you cook is almost as important as what you cook. Before you start, cut every scrap of visible fat from any meat. Joints should be pricked all over to encourage any internal fat to melt out during cooking and placed on a rack in the roasting tin. Smaller pieces of meat or fish should be grilled whenever possible. If you are frying food, non-stick pans are ideal as a light rub with a little polyunsaturated margarine or vegetable oil is all that is required to prevent food sticking. Although we mention sunflower oil throughout the book, corn, safflower or soya oils are equally suitable. Make casseroles and stews in advance so that when they have cooled, every scrap of saturated fat can be removed from the surface.

In order to help you organise your everyday menus we have used this chapter to give examples of breakfasts, four main meals and five slightly lighter lunches or suppers. With a little bit of planning and some practice, a cholesterol-lowering diet can be made tempting, varied and interesting enough to please the most critical member of the family.

Breakfasts

Don't make the mistake of missing breakfast. It provides the necessary energy to start the day and needn't throw out the balance of a cholesterol-lowering diet if you plan the menu carefully.

Chilled fruit or tomato juice makes a refreshing start, and stewed or fresh fruit is delicious on its own or stirred into some home-made low fat yogurt.

Cereals provide bulk and may be eaten with skimmed or filled milk (see page 116). As breakfast is usually eaten in a rush or in a half-awake state, it is particularly important to have a jug of this milk ready mixed in the refrigerator. It may of course also be used in tea or coffee.

If you must have a cooked breakfast, have a small portion of lean bacon or fish and make sure it is grilled rather than fried.

It is probably better not to go to work on an egg – they should be rationed on a low cholesterol diet and if you haven't eaten them for breakfast, there will be greater scope for main meals and home-baking treats.

Use a high polyunsaturated margarine such as Flora to spread on bread or toast and eat it with marmalade or honey or with yeast extract for extra protein.

The breakfast menus below should give you some ideas:

Low-fat natural yogurt with stewed fruit, tea or coffee

Chilled fruit juice, toast and marmalade, tea or coffee

Muesli with orange, tea or coffee

Kedgeree, tea or coffee

Grapefruit, honey and toast, tea or coffee

Grilled bacon and tomatoes, tea or coffee

Chilled tomato juice, bread rolls and honey, tea or coffee

Poached smoked haddock, tea or coffee

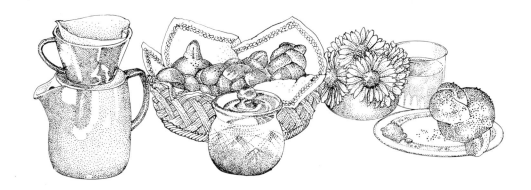

Main meals

Main Meal Menu 1

Minced beef with peppers

15 g (½ oz) Flora
1 medium onion, skinned and chopped
1 red pepper, seeded and sliced
1 green pepper, seeded and sliced
800 g (1¾ lb) lean chuck steak
15 ml (1 level tbsp) flour
300 ml (½ pint) beef stock
15 ml (1 tbsp) Worcestershire sauce
30 ml (2 level tbsp) tomato paste
2·5 ml (½ level tsp) salt
freshly ground black pepper
150 ml (¼ pint) low fat natural yogurt
chopped parsley to garnish

Melt the margarine in a large saucepan, add the onion and peppers and cook for 5 minutes. Trim any visible fat from the steak and mince it. Add the minced beef to the pan and cook for a further 5 minutes. Stir in the flour, gradually add the stock and bring to the boil, stirring continuously. Add the Worcestershire sauce, tomato paste and seasoning. Cover and cook gently for 35 minutes.

Just before serving, stir half the yogurt into the meat and reheat without boiling. Transfer the mixture to a heated serving dish, swirl the remaining yogurt over the

Autumn pudding

surface and sprinkle with parsley. Serve with boiled potatoes and baby carrots.
◗ *Calories 491 (2060)*

Autumn pudding

12 slices of starch reduced bread
225 g (8 oz) blackberries
225 g (8 oz) plums, stoned
225 g (8 oz) pears, peeled, cored and sliced
350 g (12 oz) cooking apples, peeled, cored and sliced
100 g (4 oz) soft brown sugar
150 ml ($\frac{1}{4}$ pint) water

Line a 1·4-litre (2$\frac{1}{2}$-pint) pudding basin with 8 slices of bread.

Place the fruits, sugar and water in a saucepan and simmer gently for 10 minutes until softened. Spoon into the basin and cover with the remaining slices of bread. Cover with a plate smaller in diameter than the top of the basin, place weights on top and leave to stand in a cool place for several hours, preferably overnight. Turn out and serve with natural sweetened or unsweetened yogurt.
○ *Calories 287 (1149)*

Main Meal Menu 2

Somerset lamb and vegetable layer

15 g ($\frac{1}{2}$ oz) Flora
225 g (8 oz) button onions, skinned
700 g (1$\frac{1}{2}$ lb) lean lamb
1 cooking apple, peeled, cored and diced
15 ml (1 level tbsp) flour
1·25 ml ($\frac{1}{4}$ level tsp) dried rosemary
salt and freshly ground black pepper
300 ml ($\frac{1}{2}$ pint) chicken stock
150 ml ($\frac{1}{4}$ pint) dry cider
175 g (6 oz) potato, peeled and thinly sliced
1 medium swede, peeled and thinly sliced
1 small turnip, peeled and thinly sliced
225 g (8 oz) carrot, peeled and thinly sliced
chopped parsley to garnish

Melt the margarine in a large flameproof casserole and fry the button onions for 5 minutes, until brown. Trim any visible fat from the lamb and cut into 1-cm ($\frac{1}{2}$-in) cubes. Add the meat to the pan and fry for a further 5 minutes. Add the apple, flour, rosemary and seasoning, then gradually stir in the stock and cider. Bring to the boil, stirring continuously, cover and simmer gently for 30 minutes.

Arrange a layer of potato on the top of the meat, then layers of swede, turnip and carrot. Sprinkle with salt and pepper. Cover and simmer gently for a further 1 hour. Sprinkle with parsley and serve with French or runner beans.
◗ *Calories 451 (1910)*

Rosy plum ice

5 ml (1 level tsp) powdered gelatine
75 ml (5 tbsp) hot water
300 ml ($\frac{1}{2}$ pint) filled milk (see page 116)
30 ml (2 level tbsp) caster sugar
1 567-g (1 lb 4-oz) can red plums, drained and stoned

Dissolve the gelatine in the hot water and leave to cool. Whisk the milk and sugar together and gradually whisk in the cooled gelatine. Pour into a 600-ml (1-pint) shallow container and freeze for about 1 hour until mushy.

Purée the plums in a blender or rub through a sieve. Place the frozen mixture in a large bowl and whisk until it doubles in volume. Fold in the plum purée, reserving a little to serve. Return to the shallow container and freeze until firm. Serve in individual glass dishes and spoon over the reserved plum purée. *Serves 4–6*
○ *Calories 156 (677)*

Beef toad in the hole

Main Meal Menu 3

Beef toad in the hole

350 g (12 oz) lean chuck steak
3 slices of starch reduced bread
1 small onion, skinned and finely chopped
5 ml (1 level tsp) salt
2·5 ml ($\frac{1}{2}$ level tsp) freshly ground black
  pepper
5 ml (1 tsp) chopped fresh chives
15 ml (1 level tbsp) tomato paste
1 egg white
10 ml (2 level tsp) spicy chutney
15 ml (1 tbsp) vegetable oil

For the batter
100 g (4 oz) plain flour
2·5 ml ($\frac{1}{2}$ level tsp) salt
2·5 ml ($\frac{1}{2}$ level tsp) paprika
1 egg, beaten
300 ml ($\frac{1}{2}$ pint) skimmed milk

For the batter, sift the flour, salt and paprika into a bowl, add the egg and half the milk and beat until smooth. Beat in the remaining milk.

Trim any visible fat from the steak and mince with the bread. Stir in the onion, seasoning, chives, tomato paste, egg white and chutney. Roll into small balls about the size of a walnut.

Grease a non-stick roasting tin with the oil and heat in the oven at 220°C (425°F) mark 7 until the oil is hot. Arrange the meat balls in the tin and pour over the batter. Cook at the top of the oven for about 35–40 minutes until the batter is well risen and golden brown. Serve with French beans and baby carrots.

◗ *Calories 383 (1575)*

Bananas in honey orange sauce

15 g (½ oz) Flora
15 ml (1 tbsp) clear honey
2·5 ml (½ level tsp) ground cinnamon
juice of 2 oranges
10 ml (2 level tsp) cornflour
90 ml (6 tbsp) water
3 medium bananas
15 g (½ oz) walnuts, finely chopped

Place the margarine, honey, cinnamon and orange juice in a frying pan and heat gently until the margarine has melted. Blend the cornflour and water to a smooth paste and stir into the pan. Bring to the boil, stirring continuously.

Slice the peeled bananas in half lengthways, then cut each piece in two. Add to the frying pan, cover and cook gently for 5–8 minutes until tender and coated with the glaze. Serve hot, sprinkled with the walnuts.
○ *Calories 112 (413)*

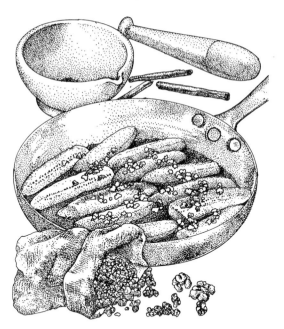

Bananas in honey
orange sauce

Main Meal Menu 4 *(illustrated in colour facing page 32)*

Honey glazed chicken

4 chicken breast portions, skinned and boned
15 g (½ oz) Flora
45 ml (3 tbsp) clear honey
300 ml (½ pint) chicken stock
1 cooking apple, cored and sliced into rings
parsley sprigs to garnish

For the stuffing
75 g (3 oz) fresh white breadcrumbs
1 small cooking apple, peeled, cored and finely
  diced
1 small onion, skinned and grated
1 stick of celery, finely chopped
1·25 ml (¼ level tsp) salt
freshly ground black pepper
5 ml (1 level tsp) dried basil
1 egg white
15 ml (1 tbsp) clear honey

Slice horizontally through the centre of each chicken breast and open out. Stir the stuffing ingredients together in a bowl and spread evenly over the chicken. Roll up the chicken breasts and secure with wooden cocktail sticks or string.

Heat the margarine and honey in a large frying pan and fry the chicken rolls gently for about 10 minutes until golden brown on all sides. Add the stock, cover and simmer gently for 30 minutes until the chicken is tender and the stock is a syrupy consistency. Transfer the chicken to a heated serving dish and remove the cocktail sticks or string. Keep hot. Add the apple slices to the remaining syrup in the frying pan and cook for 2 minutes on each side. Arrange the apple rings around the chicken, pour over the remaining syrup and garnish with the parsley sprigs. Serve with carrots and peas.
○ *Calories 462 (1835)*

Crunchy blackcurrant sundae

225 g (8 oz) fresh or frozen blackcurrants
150 ml ($\frac{1}{4}$ pint) water
75 g (3 oz) caster sugar
2 egg whites, whisked until stiff
100 g (4 oz) Nice biscuits, crushed
150 ml ($\frac{1}{4}$ pint) low fat natural yogurt
15 ml (1 tbsp) clear honey
2·5 ml ($\frac{1}{2}$ level tsp) ground cinnamon

Place the blackcurrants, water and sugar in a saucepan, bring to the boil and simmer gently for 5–10 minutes until the fruit is tender. Purée in a blender or rub through a sieve. Leave to cool, then fold in the egg whites.

Divide half the biscuit crumbs between four individual sundae dishes. Stir the yogurt, honey and cinnamon together and spoon half this mixture on top of the biscuits. Make a third layer with half the blackcurrant mixture. Repeat the layering, ending with the blackcurrant mixture, and chill well before serving.
○ *Calories 179 (702)*

Lighter meals

Lunch or Supper Menu 1

Veal and mushroom pancakes

For the batter
100 g (4 oz) plain flour
pinch salt
1 egg white
300 ml ($\frac{1}{2}$ pint) skimmed milk
15 ml (1 tbsp) vegetable oil for frying

For the filling
15 g ($\frac{1}{2}$ oz) Flora
1 small onion, skinned and chopped
100 g (4 oz) button mushrooms, sliced
30 ml (2 level tbsp) flour
300 ml ($\frac{1}{2}$ pint) skimmed milk
450 g (1 lb) lean veal, cooked and minced
salt and freshly ground pepper
75 g (3 oz) Edam cheese, grated
30 ml (2 tbsp) chopped parsley

Sift the flour and salt into a mixing bowl, make a well in the centre and add the egg white. Gradually stir in half the milk, beat thoroughly with a wooden spoon, then stir in the remaining milk. Use to make eight pancakes in the usual way.

For the filling, melt the margarine in a saucepan, add the onion and mushrooms and cook gently for 5 minutes until soft. Stir in the flour and gradually blend in the skimmed milk. Bring to the boil, stirring until thickened. Stir in the veal and seasoning and reheat gently.

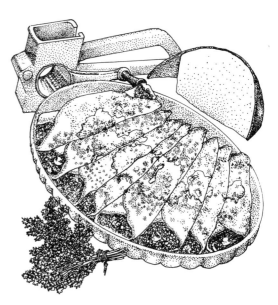

Veal and mushroom pancakes

Divide the filling evenly between the pancakes. Roll them up and arrange in a shallow flameproof dish. Sprinkle with the cheese and heat under a hot grill until the cheese has melted. Serve sprinkled with parsley.

◉ *Calories 411 (1613)*

Apricot and ginger whip

100 g (4 oz) dried apricots
300 ml ($\frac{1}{2}$ pint) water
45 ml (3 tbsp) lemon juice
30 ml (2 level tbsp) demerara sugar
5–10 ml (1–2 level tsp) ground ginger
150 ml ($\frac{1}{4}$ pint) low fat natural yogurt
2 egg whites
15 g ($\frac{1}{2}$ oz) walnuts, finely chopped

Place the apricots in a saucepan with the water, 15 ml (1 tbsp) of the lemon juice and the sugar. Cover and poach for 20–25 minutes, until the apricots are tender. Purée in an electric blender or rub through a sieve and leave to cool.

Mix the ground ginger with the yogurt and remaining lemon juice, then stir into the apricot purée. Whisk the egg whites until stiff and fold into the apricot mixture. Spoon into four individual sundae dishes and chill well. Sprinkle with the chopped walnuts just before serving.

○ *Calories 89 (338)*

Lunch or Supper Menu 2

Chicken and apple salad

1 red skinned apple, cored and diced
1 green skinned apple, cored and diced
10 ml (2 tsp) lemon juice
350 g (12 oz) lean cooked chicken meat, cubed
50 g (2 oz) lean cooked ham, diced
2 sticks of celery, washed and chopped
25 g (1 oz) sultanas
grated rind and juice of $\frac{1}{2}$ orange
150 ml ($\frac{1}{4}$ pint) low fat natural yogurt
salt and freshly ground black pepper
1 curly endive, trimmed and washed

Place the diced apples in a large bowl, add the lemon juice and stir gently until evenly coated. Add the chicken, ham, celery and sultanas.

Whisk the orange rind and juice into the yogurt and season. Add the yogurt mixture to the chicken mixture and stir gently until the salad ingredients are evenly coated. Arrange the endive on a serving dish and pile the chicken mixture in the centre. Serve with crusty bread or crispbread.

◑ *Calories 267 (1065)*

Caramel fruit condé

50 g (2 oz) pudding rice
600 ml (1 pint) skimmed milk
25 g (1 oz) sultanas
10 ml (2 level tsp) chopped mixed peel
grated rind of 1 lemon
15 ml (1 tbsp) lemon juice
150 ml ($\frac{1}{4}$ pint) lemon and orange yogurt
25 g (1 oz) caster sugar

Place the rice in a saucepan with the milk, bring to the boil, cover and simmer gently for 1$\frac{1}{2}$ hours. Remove from the heat and stir in the sultanas, peel and lemon rind. Leave to cool.

Stir the lemon juice and yogurt into the rice mixture and spoon into four 150-ml ($\frac{1}{4}$-pint) flameproof soufflé dishes. Sprinkle with the sugar and heat under a hot grill for 2–3 minutes until the sugar caramelises. Cool and chill for 30 minutes before serving.

○ *Calories 141 (555)*

Lunch or Supper Menu 3

Veal and sweetcorn risotto

15 g ($\frac{1}{2}$ oz) Flora
1 large onion, skinned and chopped
225 g (8 oz) carrots, peeled and diced
1 red pepper, seeded and chopped
700 g ($1\frac{1}{2}$ lb) lean veal
2·5 ml ($\frac{1}{2}$ level tsp) salt
1·25 ml ($\frac{1}{4}$ level tsp) freshly ground black
  pepper
300 ml ($\frac{1}{2}$ pint) chicken stock
300 ml ($\frac{1}{2}$ pint) skimmed milk
100 g (4 oz) long grain rice
326-g ($11\frac{1}{2}$-oz) can sweetcorn kernels,
  drained
50 g (2 oz) Edam cheese, grated
chopped parsley to garnish

Melt the margarine in a large saucepan, add the onion, carrots and red pepper and cook for 5 minutes until soft. Trim any visible fat from the veal and cut into 1-cm ($\frac{1}{2}$-in) cubes. Add the veal to the pan, cover and cook over a low heat for 15 minutes.

Add the seasoning, stock, milk and rice, cover and cook for 20–25 minutes until the veal and rice are tender and the liquid absorbed. Add the sweetcorn kernels for the last 5 minutes of cooking time. Turn into a heated serving dish and sprinkle with the cheese and parsley.
● *Calories 423 (1726)*

Fresh fruit and yogurt salad

1 small honeydew melon, halved and seeded
1 large grapefruit, peeled and segmented
2 large oranges, peeled and segmented
1 green eating apple, cored and sliced
1 red eating apple, cored and sliced
75 g (3 oz) black grapes, halved
300 ml ($\frac{1}{2}$ pint) mandarin and lemon yogurt

Scoop out the melon flesh with a melon baller, or cut into small cubes, and place in a large bowl. Add the grapefruit and orange segments to the melon with the apple slices and grapes. Stir in the yogurt and divide between six individual sundae dishes.
Serves 6
○ *Calories 127 (535)*

Lunch or Supper Menu 4

Cottage cheese and bacon flan

175 g (6 oz) all-in-one shortcrust pastry (see
  page 100)

For the filling
15 g ($\frac{1}{2}$ oz) Flora
1 small onion, skinned and chopped
3 rashers of lean bacon, rinded
salt and freshly ground black pepper
100 g (4 oz) cottage cheese
30 ml (2 level tbsp) skimmed milk
5 ml (1 level tsp) dry mustard
1 egg white
2 tomatoes, sliced

Roll out the pastry dough and use to line a 20·5-cm (8-in) flan ring. Bake blind in the oven at 190°C (375°F) mark 5 for 10 minutes.

For the filling, melt the margarine in a frying pan and cook the onion for 4 minutes until soft but not brown. Trim any visible fat from the bacon and chop. Add to the pan with the onion and seasoning and continue cooking for 2 minutes. In a bowl mix together the cottage cheese, milk and mustard and stir in the bacon mixture. Whisk the egg white until stiff and fold into the cottage cheese mixture. Spoon into the flan case and arrange the sliced tomatoes around the edge. Bake for 15 minutes. Serve hot or cold with a green salad.
● *Calories 481 (1830)*

Spicy hot fruit salad

3 large oranges
225 g (8 oz) fresh or frozen raspberries
2 large ripe pears, peeled, halved, cored and
    sliced
25 g (1 oz) caster sugar
90 ml (6 tbsp) water
5 ml (1 level tsp) ground cinnamon
2·5 ml (½ level tsp) ground ginger
1 banana, sliced

Peel two of the oranges and divide into segments. Place the raspberries, pears and orange segments in a saucepan. Add the sugar, water, spices, and the grated rind and juice of the remaining orange.

Cover and simmer gently for 5 minutes. Add the banana and cook for a further 3–4 minutes. Serve hot with natural yogurt or custard made with skimmed or filled milk.
○ *Calories 111 (455)*

Lunch or Supper Menu 5

Baked halibut parcels

6 175 g (6 oz) halibut or haddock cutlets
15 ml (1 tbsp) sunflower oil
40 g (1½ oz) Flora
salt and freshly ground pepper
1 lemon
450 g (1 lb) firm tomatoes, skinned, seeded
    and diced
50 g (2 oz) fresh white breadcrumbs
50 g (2 oz) Edam cheese, grated
chopped fresh chives

Lightly oil six sheets of foil large enough to wrap each cutlet. Lay the fish on the foil, dot with half the margarine, season and squeeze the juice from half the lemon over the fish. Scatter with the diced tomatoes. Seal each parcel, place on a baking sheet and cook in the oven at 170°C (325°F) mark 3 for 30 minutes.

Stir the breadcrumbs and cheese together and season. Unwrap the fish parcels and place in a flameproof dish. Spoon over the breadcrumb mixture and dot with the remaining margarine. Cook under a hot grill until golden brown. Cut the remaining half lemon into thin slices, place one on top of each cutlet and sprinkle with chives.
Serves 6
○ *Calories 388 (1567)*

Compote of raspberries with apple

50 g (2 oz) caster sugar
45 ml (3 tbsp) lemon juice
3 crisp eating apples
cinnamon stick
350 g (12 oz) fresh or frozen raspberries,
    hulled
25 g (1 oz) long thread toasted coconut

Place the sugar in a large saucepan with the lemon juice. Dissolve over a gentle heat. Peel and core the apples and thinly slice them straight into the pan. Add the cinnamon stick and raspberries. Leave over a very low heat for a few minutes until the fruit just begins to soften and the juice runs. Cool then chill in the refrigerator. Turn into a glass serving bowl and scatter with the long thread coconut. *Serves 6*
○ *Calories 101 (409)*

Menus for Healthy Entertaining

Anyone can lash cream and butter into sauces and vegetables, but menus for cholesterol-lowering entertaining can be as varied, satisfying and sophisticated as the imagination of the cook allows. All that has to be dispensed with is saturated fat, which leaves the widest possible scope for concentrating on *flavour*, *texture* and *colour*.

Even though meat should be lean and trimmed of all visible fat, and poultry should have its skin removed, any loss of flavour is more than compensated for by clever use of seasonings and fresh herbs and spices. Marinades make meat tender and succulent and aromatic stuffings flavour it from the inside out. Casseroles are always popular for dinner parties as they can be cooked well in advance. Not only does this enable every bit of saturated animal fat to be removed from the chilled casserole, but the flavour will actually improve if given time to mellow. Richly flavoured jelly stock can be chilled and skimmed in the same way.

Make use of the crunchy textures of fruit, vegetables and nuts. They are cholesterol free and make interesting and healthy garnishes – sliced apple on a salad, chopped chives scattered over boiled new potatoes, toasted almonds on a fruit mousse. In their own right, a selection of slightly under-cooked vegetables attractively arranged on a platter combines crispness of texture with bright, contrasting colours. The rule about never serving an 'all-white' or an 'all-red' meal is more important than ever when cooking cholesterol-lowering dishes for guests.

There are plenty of interesting alternatives to the banned heavy fats. Cream and egg yolks can be replaced in sauces and casseroles by a spoonful or two of natural low fat yogurt, and while the richer fats often make flavours more bland, yogurt adds a fresh tangy taste of its own. In savoury dishes, puréed vegetables add body without making a dish heavy or cloying. A soft margarine like Flora, high in poly-unsaturates, can be treated like butter and flavoured with lemon, garlic, parsley, curry, etc. These small pats of savoury 'butter' should be kept in the refrigerator until required, then used to add flavour and interest to baked potatoes, grilled meats and fish and vegetables.

When it is your turn to be a guest at

someone else's house, do warn your hostess in advance so that she doesn't start to think in terms of roast pork and creamy desserts. If this is not possible, you can at least refuse butter and cream. In a restaurant, it is easy enough to follow the same principles you would at home. Choose a clear soup or a fruit or vegetable based starter, avoiding anything likely to be coated in mayonnaise or dressed with vinaigrette. Some sort of plainly cooked fish, poultry or meat should be available on any menu and all you must do is to remove any fat before you eat it and avoid gravy or rich cream sauces. Steer clear of made up dishes, pies and anything fried. Choose fresh fruit or a sorbet for dessert and have black coffee to round off the meal.

To guide you and to help you produce a delicious, sophisticated *and* healthy meal at home, take a look at the eleven menus we have compiled for you. There are the lunches and dinners you would expect, but it may surprise you to learn that you can organise a barbecue, sit down to an Indian feast, prepare a Chinese meal and produce a buffet for a large family gathering – all without breaking any of the healthy eating rules. You will never need to apologise or explain, and if they realise at all, your guests will be delighted that you cook the cholesterol-lowering way.

Menu 1 : Dinner Party for 6

Smoked cod salad	*Braised veal in sherry*	*Melon and wine jelly*
	Sesame broccoli	*Coffee fluff with mandarin oranges*
	Golden potato wedges	

Prepare the Smoked cod salad in advance, omitting the apple, and assemble just before serving. The veal and the Golden potato wedges are cooked together in the oven at the same temperature.

Make the two desserts in plenty of time for them to become thoroughly chilled and set, but preferably not the day before the dinner as the jelly will become rubbery.

Smoked cod salad

100 g (4 oz) long grain rice
30 ml (2 tbsp) wine vinegar
60 ml (4 tbsp) sunflower oil
2·5 ml ($\frac{1}{2}$ level tsp) made mustard
salt and freshly ground black pepper
2 red skinned eating apples, cored
juice of $\frac{1}{2}$ lemon
2 sticks of celery, washed and sliced
700 g (1$\frac{1}{2}$ lb) cooked smoked cod, flaked
1 curly endive, trimmed and washed
parsley sprigs to garnish

Cook the rice in boiling salted water for 10–12 minutes until tender. Drain well. Whisk together the vinegar, oil, mustard and seasoning and pour over the rice while still warm. Leave to cool.

Cut one of the apples into slices and the other into small dice and toss in the lemon juice. Stir the diced apple into the cold rice with the celery and fish and mix well. Arrange the endive on six individual plates and spoon the fish salad into the centre. Chill before serving, garnished with the apple slices and with parsley sprigs. *Serves 6*
◑ *Calories 216 (902)*

Braised veal in sherry

1·4 kg (3 lb) lean breast of veal
25 g (1 oz) Flora
225 g (8 oz) carrots, peeled and sliced
225 g (8 oz) leeks, sliced and washed
225 g (8 oz) button onions, skinned
4 sticks of celery, sliced
25 g (1 oz) flour
30 ml (2 level tbsp) tomato paste
400 ml ($\frac{3}{4}$ pint) chicken stock
150 ml ($\frac{1}{4}$ pint) dry sherry
salt and freshly ground black pepper
1 bay leaf
2·5 ml ($\frac{1}{2}$ level tsp) dried mixed herbs
225 g (8 oz) courgettes, trimmed and sliced
100 g (4 oz) button mushrooms

For the stuffing
50 g (2 oz) Flora
1 small onion, skinned and chopped
50 g (2 oz) mushrooms, chopped
2 sticks of celery, chopped
50 g (2 oz) fresh white breadcrumbs
25 g (1 oz) seedless raisins
little beaten egg white to bind
salt and freshly ground pepper

For the stuffing, melt the margarine in a frying pan and fry the onion for 5 minutes until soft. Add the mushrooms and celery and fry for a further 5 minutes. Stir in the breadcrumbs, raisins, egg white and seasoning. Spread the stuffing over one side of the veal, roll up neatly and tie securely with string.

Melt the margarine in a large frying pan, add the carrots, leeks, onions and celery and cook for 5 minutes. Place in a 2-litre ($3\frac{1}{2}$-pint) ovenproof casserole. Add the veal to the pan and fry for 10 minutes until brown on all sides; add to the casserole. Stir the flour and tomato paste into the pan and cook for 2 minutes. Gradually add the stock and sherry and bring to the boil, stirring until thickened. Season and pour over the veal in the casserole. Add the bay leaf and mixed herbs.

Cover and cook in the oven at 180°C (350°F) mark 4 for $2\frac{1}{2}$ hours. Add the courgettes and mushrooms and continue cooking for a further 30 minutes. Transfer the veal to a heated serving dish and remove the string. Surround with the vegetables and a little of the sauce. Serve the remaining sauce separately. *Serves 6*
◑ *Calories 770 (3255)*

Sesame broccoli

150 ml ($\frac{1}{4}$ pint) water
1·1 kg ($2\frac{1}{2}$ lb) broccoli, trimmed and divided into sprigs
20 ml (4 tsp) soy sauce
salt and freshly ground black pepper
40 g ($1\frac{1}{2}$ oz) Flora
10 ml (2 level tsp) sesame seeds

Bring the water to the boil in a large saucepan and add the broccoli, soy sauce and seasoning. Cover and cook for 15 minutes until just tender. Drain broccoli thoroughly. Add margarine, sprinkle over the sesame seeds and turn gently to coat the broccoli without breaking the florets. Spoon into a heated serving dish. *Serves 6*
○ *Calories 83 (313)*

Golden potato wedges

6 medium potatoes, peeled
15 ml (1 tbsp) sunflower oil
salt

Cut each potato in half lengthways, then cut each half into three wedges. Place the wedges in a single layer in a large roasting tin. Brush the potatoes with oil and sprinkle with salt. Bake in the oven at 180°C (350°F) mark 4 for 45 minutes until crisp and golden brown. *Serves 6*
○ *Calories 141 (597)*

Melon and wine jelly

15 g ($\frac{1}{2}$ oz) powdered gelatine
45 ml (3 tbsp) boiling water
300 ml ($\frac{1}{2}$ pint) cold water
50 g (2 oz) caster sugar
300 ml ($\frac{1}{2}$ pint) dry red wine
1 ripe honeydew melon, halved and seeded

Family main meal *(page 25)*: Honey glazed chicken, Crunchy blackcurrant sundae ▶

Dissolve the gelatine in the boiling water in a small bowl. In a saucepan gently heat the cold water and sugar, stirring to dissolve the sugar. Stir in the gelatine and wine and leave to cool.

Meanwhile, cut the melon into balls with a parisienne cutter. Pour a little of the wine mixture into six individual glass dishes and leave to set. Add a layer of melon balls, pour over the remaining wine mixture and leave to set. Top the jellies with the remaining melon balls and chill thoroughly. *Serves 6* ○ *Calories 85 (342)*

Coffee fluff with mandarin oranges

1 egg, beaten
50 g (2 oz) soft brown sugar
300 ml (½ pint) skimmed milk
5 ml (1 level tsp) instant coffee granules
60 ml (4 tbsp) boiling water
15 g (½ oz) powdered gelatine
10 ml (2 tsp) rum
3 egg whites
312-g (11-oz) can mandarin oranges, drained

Beat the egg and sugar together in a bowl. Heat the milk to boiling point and pour on to the egg mixture, stirring. Return the custard to the pan and cook over a gentle heat, stirring, until thickened.

Dissolve the coffee granules in 15 ml (1 tbsp) of the boiling water and the gelatine in the remaining boiling water. Stir the dissolved coffee and gelatine into the custard with the rum. Cover with a piece of dampened greaseproof paper and leave to cool. Just before the custard sets, whisk the egg whites until stiff and gently fold into the custard. Pour the mixture into six individual glass dishes and leave to set thoroughly. Decorate with mandarin segments. *Serves 6* ○ *Calories 85 (338)*

Menu 2 : Dinner Party for 4

Mushroom and lemon soup   *Cheesy veal escalopes with noodles*   *Burgundy peaches*
Melba toast   *Courgettes in tomato sauce*

Prepare the Mushroom and lemon soup in advance and reheat just before serving. The Melba toast can also be reheated under a low grill.

The veal escalopes have to be cooked at the last minute but can be coated in egg and breadcrumbs and stored, covered, in the refrigerator until required.

Burgundy peaches are delicious well chilled, but why not take the opportunity of serving a hot dessert, keeping the peaches warm in a very low oven.

Mushroom and lemon soup

25 g (1 oz) Flora
1 medium onion, skinned and sliced
450 g (1 lb) button mushrooms
600 ml (1 pint) chicken stock
300 ml (½ pint) skimmed milk
5 ml (1 level tsp) salt
freshly ground black pepper
1 lemon
5 ml (1 level tsp) caster sugar

Melt the margarine in a large saucepan and fry the onion gently for 5 minutes. Add the

Dinner party for six *(page 46)*: Devilled mushrooms, Veal escalopes in cider sauce, Tutti frutti pineapple rings

mushrooms and fry for 5 minutes. Stir in the stock, milk and seasoning, cover and simmer gently for 25 minutes.

Purée the soup in a blender or rub through a sieve. Return to the pan and reheat gently. Cut the lemon in half and add the grated rind and juice of one half to the soup with the sugar. Stir well. Cut the other half of the lemon into thin slices. Serve soup in heated bowls and float the lemon slices on top.

○ *Calories 108 (418)*

Cheesy veal escalopes with noodles

4 225-g (8-oz) veal escalopes
20 ml (4 level tsp) made mustard
100 g (4 oz) Edam cheese, grated
salt and freshly ground white pepper
25 g (1 oz) flour
2 egg whites, lightly beaten
15 ml (1 tbsp) chopped fresh rosemary
100 g (4 oz) fresh white breadcrumbs
30 ml (2 tbsp) sunflower oil
25 g (1 oz) Flora
225 g (8 oz) noodles
sprigs of parsley to garnish

Trim any visible fat from the meat, place between sheets of greaseproof paper and beat out until thin with a meat mallet or rolling pin. Spread with the mustard and sprinkle over the cheese and seasoning. Fold each escalope in half and secure the open sides with wooden cocktail sticks. Coat the veal in flour and dip in the egg white. Stir the rosemary and breadcrumbs together and use to coat the escalopes. Heat the oil and margarine in a large frying pan and fry the escalopes for 6 minutes on each side until golden brown.

Meanwhile, cook the noodles in a pan of boiling salted water for 12–15 minutes. Drain and place in a heated deep serving dish. Arrange the veal escalopes on top of the noodles, remove the cocktail sticks and garnish with sprigs of parsley.

● *Calories 641 (2541)*

Courgettes in tomato sauce

30 ml (2 tbsp) sunflower oil
1 clove of garlic, skinned and crushed
900 g (2 lb) courgettes, trimmed and sliced
30 ml (2 level tbsp) tomato paste
salt and freshly ground black pepper
225 g (8 oz) tomatoes, skinned, seeded and chopped
300 ml ($\frac{1}{2}$ pint) chicken stock
10 ml (2 level tsp) cornflour

Heat the oil in a large frying pan, add the garlic and courgettes and fry for 3 minutes. Stir in the tomato paste, seasoning, tomatoes and stock. Bring to the boil, cover and simmer gently for 12 minutes.

Blend the cornflour to a smooth paste with a little water and stir into the pan. Bring to the boil, stirring, and cook for 2 minutes. Transfer to a heated serving dish.

○ *Calories 114 (476)*

Burgundy peaches

1 orange
1 lemon
100 g (4 oz) caster sugar
150 ml ($\frac{1}{4}$ pint) water
$\frac{1}{2}$ cinnamon stick
1 clove
300 ml ($\frac{1}{2}$ pint) red burgundy wine
4 large peaches, skinned, halved and stoned
15 ml (1 level tbsp) arrowroot

Cut the rind from the orange, then squeeze out the juice. Remove one strip of rind from the lemon. Place the sugar, water, cinnamon stick, clove and orange juice in a large frying pan. Add the strip of lemon rind and a similar sized piece of the orange rind. Cover and bring to the boil. Add the wine and fruit and simmer for 20 minutes.

Meanwhile, remove any remaining pith from a 5-cm (2-in) strip of orange rind and cut into very thin strips. Place in a small pan and cover with water. Bring to the boil, then poach for 20 minutes and drain. Spoon the peaches into a serving dish (heated if you plan to serve this as a hot dessert). Blend the arrowroot to a smooth

paste with a little water and stir into the wine mixture. Bring to the boil, stirring until thickened. Strain the wine sauce over the peaches and scatter with the strips of orange rind. Serve hot or well chilled.
○ *Calories 231 (927)*

Menu 3 : Dinner Party for 4

Chilled leeks in red wine
Melba toast

Tarragon steaks with mushrooms
Carrot and celery julienne
Parsley rice

Apple and orange liqueur fools

Prepare the leeks and make the Melba toast in advance, reheating the toast under a low grill at the last minute. Cut the Carrot and celery julienne strips and store in an air-tight container until ready to cook them. Prepare the Apple and orange liqueur fools well in advance, but don't add the flaked almonds until just before serving.

Chilled leeks in red wine

30 ml (2 tbsp) sunflower oil
450 g (1 lb) leeks, trimmed, sliced and washed
salt and freshly ground black pepper
150 ml ($\frac{1}{4}$ pint) dry red wine
30 ml (2 tbsp) beef stock

Tarragon steaks
with mushrooms

Heat the oil in a frying pan, add the leeks and seasoning and fry for 2 minutes. Pour over the wine and stock, cover and simmer gently for 10 minutes. Spoon the leeks into a serving dish. Bring the liquid in the pan to the boil and boil for 2 minutes until slightly reduced. Pour the liquid over the leeks and chill well. Serve with Melba toast.
○ *Calories 113 (476)*

Tarragon steaks with mushrooms

15 g ($\frac{1}{2}$ oz) Flora
15 ml (1 tbsp) sunflower oil
4 225-g (8-oz) sirloin steaks
150 ml ($\frac{1}{4}$ pint) beef stock
300 ml ($\frac{1}{2}$ pint) dry white wine
175 g (6 oz) button mushrooms, sliced
30 ml (2 tbsp) chopped fresh tarragon
salt and freshly ground black pepper
15 ml (1 level tbsp) cornflour
watercress to garnish

Heat the margarine and oil in a large frying pan. Trim all visible fat from the steaks and fry for 2 minutes on each side. Pour in the stock and wine. Add the mushrooms, tarragon and seasoning, cover and simmer gently for 5 minutes. Remove the steaks to a heated serving dish, cover and keep warm.

Blend the cornflour to a smooth paste with a little water and add to the wine stock. Bring to the boil, stirring, and cook for 3 minutes until thickened. Pour over the steaks and garnish with watercress.
◑ *Calories 524 (2173)*

Carrot and celery julienne

450 g (1 lb) carrots, peeled
1 head of celery, trimmed and washed
25 g (1 oz) Flora
5 ml (1 level tsp) salt
freshly ground black pepper
60 ml (4 tbsp) beef stock
chopped parsley to garnish

Cut the carrots and celery into 5-cm (2-in) matchstick lengths (julienne strips). Melt the margarine in a large frying pan, add the vegetables and fry gently for 5 minutes. Add the seasoning and stock, cover and simmer for 15 minutes. Spoon into a heated serving dish and garnish with parsley.
○ *Calories 81 (321)*

Parsley rice

225 g (8 oz) long grain rice
salt and freshly ground white pepper
45 ml (3 tbsp) chopped parsley

Cook the rice in a pan of boiling salted water for 12–15 minutes until tender. Drain and rinse with boiling water. Season and stir in the parsley. Spoon into a heated serving dish.
○ *Calories 70 (284)*

Apple and orange liqueur fools

700 g (1½ lb) cooking apples, peeled, cored and sliced
45 ml (3 tbsp) water
30 ml (2 level tbsp) caster sugar
grated rind and juice of 1 orange
60 ml (4 tbsp) orange-flavoured liqueur, such as Cointreau or Grand Marnier
150 ml (¼ pint) low fat natural yogurt
1 egg white
toasted flaked almonds to decorate

Place the apples in a saucepan with the water. Cover and simmer gently for 15 minutes until soft. Purée in a blender or rub through a sieve. Stir in the sugar, orange rind and juice, liqueur and yogurt. Whisk the egg white until stiff and fold into the apple mixture. Spoon the fool into four individual glass dishes and chill for 20 minutes before serving. Decorate with toasted flaked almonds.
○ *Calories 118 (501)*

Menu 4 : Barbecue for 6

Thick vegetable soup	*Beef and lamb kebabs*	*Fresh fruit kebabs*
	Spicy barbecue sauce	
	Avocado and grapefruit salad	
	Chilli bean salad	
	Mushroom rice salad	

Remember to light the barbecue about 1 hour before you want to start cooking, allowing the charcoal to burn until the embers glow red (or white if cooking in daylight). If the weather suddenly changes, the kebabs will be just as enjoyable cooked under an ordinary grill!

Have the vegetable soup and the Spicy barbecue sauce prepared, ready to reheat before serving. Thread the meat and the fruit kebabs on to their skewers and keep in the refrigerator, covered tightly with cling film, until required.

Prepare the salads in advance, but follow the recipe directions about the stage at which they should be assembled.

Thick vegetable soup

25 g (1 oz) Flora
3 large carrots, peeled and sliced
1 large onion, skinned and chopped
225 g (8 oz) swede, peeled and chopped
1 small turnip, peeled and chopped
2 small potatoes, peeled and chopped
3 sticks of celery, washed and sliced
1·2 litres (2 pints) chicken stock
5 ml (1 level tsp) salt
freshly ground black pepper
30 ml (2 level tbsp) tomato paste
2·5 ml (½ level tsp) dried mixed herbs
15 ml (1 tbsp) chopped parsley

Melt the margarine in a large saucepan, add the vegetables and fry for 10 minutes. Add the stock, seasoning, tomato paste and mixed herbs. Bring to the boil, cover and simmer for 45–50 minutes, until the vegetables are tender.

Purée the soup in a blender or rub through a sieve. Return to a clean saucepan and reheat. Serve sprinkled with chopped parsley. *Serves 6*
○ *Calories 106 (418)*

Beef and lamb kebabs

700 g (1½ lb) lean rump steak
225 g (8 oz) lean lamb
1 small red pepper, seeded
1 large cooking apple, peeled and cored
12 small firm tomatoes, or 6 larger ones, halved
salt and freshly ground black pepper
60 ml (4 tbsp) vegetable oil

Trim all visible fat from the meat and cut into 2·5-cm (1-in) cubes. Cut the pepper and apple into 2·5-cm (1-in) pieces. Divide the ingredients between six long skewers. Sprinkle each kebab with seasoning and brush with oil.

Cook over the prepared barbecue (or under a hot grill) for 20–25 minutes, turning the kebabs frequently and brushing with oil. Serve with Spicy barbecue sauce. *Serves 6*
◗ *Calories 426 (1797)*

Spicy barbecue sauce

25 g (1 oz) Flora
1 large onion, skinned and finely chopped
1 red pepper, seeded and finely chopped
1 clove of garlic, skinned and crushed
2·5 ml (½ level tsp) chilli powder
2·5 ml (½ tsp) Tabasco sauce
10 ml (2 tsp) Worcestershire sauce
grated rind of 1 lemon
15 ml (1 level tbsp) redcurrant jelly
pinch sugar
150 ml (¼ pint) dry cider
400 ml (¾ pint) beef stock

Melt the margarine in a large saucepan and fry the onion, pepper and garlic for 5 minutes. Add the remaining ingredients, bring to the boil, cover and simmer for 20 minutes. *Serves 6*
○ *Calories 81 (263)*

Avocado and grapefruit salad

1 eating apple, peeled, cored and diced
2 large avocados, peeled, stoned and sliced
lemon juice
1 cos lettuce, washed and finely shredded
1 bunch of watercress, washed and chopped
2 sticks of celery, washed and sliced
25 g (1 oz) sultanas

For the dressing
1 grapefruit, peeled
15 ml (1 tbsp) lemon juice
30 ml (2 tbsp) vegetable oil
15 ml (1 tbsp) white wine vinegar
salt and freshly ground black pepper
10 ml (2 level tsp) caster sugar

For the dressing, divide the grapefruit into segments (over a bowl to catch the juices) add the remaining ingredients to the juice and whisk together. Reserve the segments.

Turn the apple and avocados in a little lemon juice to prevent discoloration and assemble all the salad ingredients, including the grapefruit segments, in a large bowl. Just before serving pour over the dressing, toss until evenly coated and turn into a serving dish. *Serves 6*
○ *Calories 88 (363)*

Chilli bean salad

2 medium onions, skinned and sliced
1 red pepper, seeded and sliced
1 green pepper, seeded and sliced
4 large tomatoes, skinned, seeded and
  quartered
425-g (15-oz) can red kidney beans, drained
15 ml (1 tbsp) chopped fresh chives
1 head of chicory, trimmed and chopped

For the dressing
30 ml (2 tbsp) vegetable oil
15 ml (1 tbsp) chilli vinegar
2·5 ml ($\frac{1}{2}$ tsp) Tabasco sauce
pinch of chilli powder
salt and freshly ground black pepper
pinch of sugar

Blanch the sliced onions and peppers in boiling water for 5 minutes. Drain and rinse under cold water. Place in a large bowl and stir in the tomatoes, kidney beans and chives.

Whisk the dressing ingredients together and pour over the bean mixture. Toss until evenly coated. Place the chicory on the bottom of the serving dish and spoon in the kidney bean mixture. Chill for 1–2 hours before serving. *Serves 6*
○ *Calories 125 (509)*

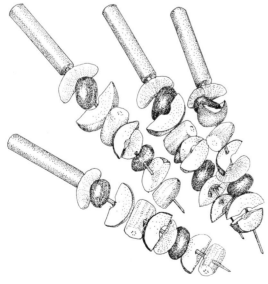

Fresh fruit kebabs

Mushroom rice salad

15 g ($\frac{1}{2}$ oz) Flora
450 g (1 lb) button mushrooms, sliced
225 g (8 oz) long grain rice, cooked
1 cucumber, diced
50 g (2 oz) walnuts, chopped
1 lettuce, washed and shredded

For the dressing
10 ml (2 tsp) lemon juice
15 ml (1 level tbsp) curry paste
30 ml (2 tbsp) low fat natural yogurt
salt and freshly ground black pepper

Melt the margarine in a saucepan and fry the mushrooms for 3 minutes. Cool. Place the rice in a large bowl with the cucumber, walnuts and mushrooms. Stir until well mixed. Whisk the dressing ingredients together until well blended. Pour over the salad ingredients and turn until well coated.

Put the lettuce in a serving dish. Just before serving spoon the mushroom mixture on top. *Serves 6*
○ *Calories 138 (535)*

Fresh fruit kebabs

2 large oranges, peeled and segmented
125 g (4 oz) fresh dates, stoned
3 large peaches, stoned and quartered
2 medium bananas, quartered
2 green apples, cored and quartered

For the syrup
90 ml (6 tbsp) water
30 ml (2 level tbsp) sugar
15 ml (1 level tbsp) clear honey
5 ml (1 level tsp) mixed spice

Mix the syrup ingredients together in a small saucepan. Heat gently until the sugar has dissolved, then boil for 4–5 minutes, until a syrupy consistency.

Thread the fruit on to six skewers. Brush the fruit with the syrup and cook over the prepared barbecue (or under a hot grill) for 10–12 minutes, turning and basting frequently with the syrup. *Serves 6*
○ *Calories 171 (718)*

Menu 5 : Indian Dinner Party for 6

Tandoori chicken	*Naans*	*Lemon liqueur water ice*
Seekh kebabs	*Kitchri*	
	Cucumber raita	
	Avial (Aviyal)	

Cook this authentic Indian meal at home and impress your friends.

The Lemon liqueur water ice will cool down over-heated palates and can be prepared the day before or even further in advance.

Allow 24 hours for the Tandoori chicken to marinate in the spicy mixture. The Seekh kebabs can also be prepared and shaped the day before and stored, covered with cling film, in the refrigerator. Have the naans ready to reheat in the oven during the last 15 minutes of cooking the Tandoori chicken.

The three vegetable dishes are simple enough to make while the Tandoori chicken is cooking, but do remember to soak the lentils and rice for Kitchri for 1 hour before cooking.

Tandoori chicken

1·4-kg (3-lb) oven-ready chicken
10 ml (2 level tsp) chilli powder
5 ml (1 level tsp) salt
2·5 ml (½ level tsp) freshly ground black pepper
30 ml (2 tbsp) lemon juice
50 g (2 oz) Flora

For the marinade
45 ml (3 tbsp) low fat natural yogurt
4 cloves of garlic, skinned and crushed
5-cm (2-in) piece of fresh root ginger, peeled and chopped
5 ml (1 level tsp) ground cumin
15 ml (1 level tbsp) ground coriander
5 ml (1 level tsp) paprika
2·5 ml (½ level tsp) ground turmeric
2·5 ml (½ level tsp) ground cinnamon

Pierce the flesh of the chicken all over with a sharp, thin skewer or needle. Sprinkle salt inside the bird. Stir together the chilli powder, salt, pepper and lemon juice. Rub this well into the chicken flesh and leave for 20 minutes.

Blend all the marinade ingredients to form a smooth paste. Place the chicken on a wide shallow plate or dish and spread over the marinade, again rubbing well into the flesh. Cover and refrigerate for 24 hours.

Place the chicken on a cooling rack or small grill pan rack standing in a roasting tin containing 2·5 cm (1 in) cold water. Spoon over any remaining marinade and dot with pieces of margarine. Roast the chicken at 200°C (400°F) mark 6 for about 1 hour until tender, basting frequently with the liquid in the tin. Serve the bird carved or jointed. *Serves 6*
○ *Calories 317 (1312)*

Seekh kebabs

700 g (1½ lb) raw lean lamb or beef, finely minced
1 large onion, skinned and grated
2 cloves of garlic, skinned and crushed
1 green chilli, seeded and finely chopped
7·5 ml (1½ level tsp) ground cumin
5 ml (1 level tsp) salt
5 ml (1 level tsp) black pepper
grated rind and juice of 1 lemon
60 ml (4 tbsp) vegetable oil

Thoroughly blend together all the ingredients except the oil, cover and chill for at least 1 hour. Lightly grease six flat skewers. Divide the meat mixture into 24, shape each piece into a thin strip about 10 cm (4 in) long and then roll up. Thread four meat rolls on each skewer and brush lightly with the oil. Place under a hot grill and grill for about 10 minutes, turning frequently until evenly browned. *Serves 6*
◗ *Calories 207 (886)*

Naans

A traditional yeasted flat bread to serve with the Tandoori chicken.

about 200 ml (⅓ pint) milk
7·5 ml (1½ level tsp) dried yeast
450 g (1 lb) plain white flour
2·5 ml (½ level tsp) salt
1 egg, beaten
10 ml (2 level tsp) caster sugar
5 ml (1 level tsp) baking powder
30 ml (2 tbsp) sunflower oil
60 ml (4 tbsp) low fat natural yogurt

Grease three large baking sheets. Warm 150 ml (¼ pint) of the milk to blood heat and pour into a small bowl. Sprinkle in the dried yeast and leave in a warm place for about 10–15 minutes to become really frothy. Sift together the flour and salt into a large bowl. Blend all the other ingredients, except the rest of the milk, with the yogurt. Add the yeast to the blended yogurt mixture then add this mixture to the flour. Mix well to form a soft dough, adding more of the milk if required. Knead well for 10 minutes, then cover with lightly oiled polythene and leave to rise in a warm place until doubled in size. (Alternatively, make the dough the day before and leave to rise overnight in an oiled polythene bag in the refrigerator.)

If the dough has been risen in the refrigerator allow it to come to room temperature for about 1 hour. Knead the dough for several minutes, then divide into six equal pieces. Roll out each piece on a well-floured surface and shape into an oval about 25 cm (10 in) long. Place two of these on each greased baking sheet, cover with lightly oiled polythene and leave in a warm place for 15 minutes.

Brush the centre of each naan with a little water and cook under a hot grill for 2–3 minutes on each side until golden brown and puffed up. Watch carefully to make sure they don't catch fire as they rise. Serve while still warm. *Makes 6*
○ *Calories 366 (1508)*

Kitchri

This is one of the many versions of the lentil and rice dish from which originated the Anglo-Indian equivalent, Kedgeree. Either serve it with the Seekh kebabs, or use it as a base to mop up the juices from the Avial.

100 g (4 oz) red lentils
225 g (8 oz) long grain rice
25 g (1 oz) Flora
1 onion, skinned and chopped
1 clove of garlic, skinned and crushed
600 ml (1 pint) water
1 bay leaf
2·5 ml (½ level tsp) ground turmeric
2·5 ml (½ level tsp) ground ginger
2·5 ml (½ level tsp) salt
1·25 ml (¼ level tsp) black pepper

Place the lentils and rice in a bowl, cover with cold water and leave for 1 hour. Drain well. Melt the margarine and gently fry the onion and garlic for 5 minutes. Add the drained lentils and rice and stir well. Add the measured water and seasonings, bring to the boil and simmer, covered, for 15–20 minutes until the water is absorbed and the rice and lentils cooked. Before serving, extra margarine and fried onion may be stirred into the Kitchri to give it added taste and richness. *Serves 6*
○ *Calories 107 (422)*

Cucumber raita

This is a cool, fresh-tasting accompaniment to spicy food.

225 g (8 oz) cucumber, finely diced
1 onion, skinned and finely chopped
1 clove of garlic, skinned and crushed
300 ml (½ pint) low fat natural yogurt
2·5 ml (½ level tsp) salt
1·25 ml (¼ level tsp) freshly ground black pepper

Mix the cucumber thoroughly with the remaining ingredients, cover and chill for at least 1 hour. Before serving, stir and transfer to a clean bowl. *Serves 6*
○ *Calories 30 (121)*

Avial (Aviyal)

A mild vegetable curry with an interesting texture.

5 ml (1 level tsp) mustard seeds
1 onion, skinned and finely chopped
1 green chilli, seeded and finely chopped
5 ml (1 level tsp) ground turmeric
15 ml (1 level tbsp) ground coriander
60 ml (4 tbsp) sunflower oil
450 g (1 lb) mixed vegetables, prepared and
   sliced (choose from aubergine, carrots,
   beans, cauliflower, green pepper, okra,
   potatoes, tomatoes)
5 ml (1 level tsp) salt
100 g (4 oz) fresh grated coconut
150 ml ($\frac{1}{4}$ pint) low fat natural yogurt
25 g (1 oz) Flora, melted

Gently fry the mustard seeds, onion, chilli and spices in the oil. Add the prepared vegetables, the salt and sufficient water just to keep the vegetables moist. Cook until the vegetables are tender but still crisp. Stir in the coconut and simmer for a further 5 minutes. Stir in the yogurt and melted margarine and reheat without boiling.
Serves 6
○ *Calories 217 (907)*

Lemon liqueur water ice

150 g (5 oz) caster sugar
300 ml ($\frac{1}{2}$ pint) water
2 lemons
5 ml (1 tsp) Galliano
1 egg white
angelica leaves to garnish

Place the sugar in a pan with the water and heat gently until the sugar has dissolved.

Lemon liqueur water ice

Remove two strips of rind from the lemons, add to the syrup and bring to the boil. Boil gently for 5 minutes, then leave to cool and remove the lemon rind. Squeeze the juice from the lemons and add to the syrup with the Galliano. Pour into a shallow container and freeze for about 1 hour until mushy.

Turn the mixture into a bowl and whisk until smooth. Whisk the egg white until stiff, fold into the lemon mixture and return to the container to re-freeze until firm. Spoon into individual glass dishes, decorate with angelica leaves and serve. *Serves 6*
○ *Calories 101 (443)*

Menu 6 : Dinner Party for 6

Salmon gratiné *Poussins with sultana stuffing* *Apricot meringue basket*
Scalloped potatoes *Coffee semolina mousse*
French beans

Prepare the stuffing for the poussins in advance but stuff just before cooking.

For scalloped potatoes, peel and slice 5–6 potatoes and arrange in layers in an oven-proof dish. Season each layer and sprinkle with a little flour and dot with Flora, using altogether 25 g (1 oz) of each. Pour over 150 ml ($\frac{1}{4}$ pint) skimmed milk and bake in the oven with the poussins for $1\frac{1}{4}$ hours.

Prepare both the desserts in advance but do not add the filling to the meringue basket until just before serving. The meringue can be made and stored in an airtight tin.

Salmon gratiné

50 g (2 oz) Flora
1 medium onion, skinned and finely chopped
3 sticks of celery, washed and finely chopped
45 ml (3 level tbsp) flour
300 ml ($\frac{1}{2}$ pint) skimmed milk
225-g (8-oz) can red salmon, flaked
100 g (4 oz) Edam cheese, grated
salt and freshly ground pepper
juice of $\frac{1}{2}$ lemon
50 g (2 oz) fresh white breadcrumbs

Melt the margarine in a saucepan, add the onion and celery, cover and cook gently for 10–15 minutes until tender. Add the flour and cook for 2 minutes, stirring. Gradually add the milk and bring to the boil. Cook gently for 2–3 minutes, then remove from the heat.

Add the salmon to the pan with any juice from the can. Add half the cheese, the seasoning, lemon juice and breadcrumbs and stir gently until blended. Divide the mixture between six 150-ml ($\frac{1}{4}$-pint) oven-proof dishes and sprinkle with the remaining cheese. Bake in the oven at 190°C (375°F) mark 5 for 15–20 minutes until golden brown. *Serves 6*
◗ *Calories 242 (936)*

Poussins with sultana stuffing

6 poussins
vegetable oil
45 ml (3 level tbsp) flour
300 ml ($\frac{1}{2}$ pint) chicken stock
30 ml (2 level tbsp) redcurrant jelly
juice of 1 orange
$\frac{1}{2}$ bunch of watercress

For the stuffing
100 g (4 oz) brown rice
50 g (2 oz) sultanas
2 oranges
1 medium onion, skinned and grated
30 ml (2 tbsp) chopped parsley
15 ml (1 tbsp) chopped fresh thyme or 5 ml
   (1 level tsp) dried thyme
salt and freshly ground pepper

For the stuffing, cook the brown rice in boiling salted water for about 45 minutes until tender. Add the sultanas for the last 10–15 minutes of cooking. Meanwhile, grate the rind of the two oranges and squeeze the juice of one. Drain the rice well and add the remaining ingredients, including the orange rind and juice. Stir the stuffing until all the ingredients are thoroughly blended.

Divide the stuffing and fill the cavity of each bird. Tie their legs together to keep them a good shape while cooking. Place the birds in a roasting tin and brush the breast of each with a little oil. Roast in the oven at 190°C (375°F) mark 5 for about $1\frac{1}{4}$ hours until golden brown.

Remove the poussins to a heated serving dish and keep warm. Drain the fat from the roasting tin and spoon 30 ml (2 tbsp) of the juices into a small saucepan. Stir in the flour and cook over a gentle heat until golden brown. Stir in the stock, redcurrant jelly, orange juice and seasoning. Bring to the boil, stirring, and cook for 1–2 minutes.

Garnish the poussins with the watercress and serve the sauce separately. *Serves 6*
○ *Calories 473 (1993)*

Apricot meringue basket

3 egg whites
75 g (3 oz) caster sugar
grated chocolate to decorate

For the filling
2 550-g (1 lb 4-oz) cans apricots in water, drained
50 g (2 oz) caster sugar
15 ml (1 tbsp) lemon juice
300 ml ($\frac{1}{2}$ pint) low fat natural yogurt

Line a baking sheet with non-stick paper. Whisk the egg whites until they stand in peaks. Add half the sugar and whisk again until stiff and shiny. Fold in the remaining sugar with a metal spoon or spatula. Spoon the meringue into a large icing bag fitted with a large rosette nozzle. Pipe a meringue basket, 18-cm (7-in) in diameter, on the baking sheet. Dry out in the oven at 110°C (225°F) mark $\frac{1}{4}$ for about 3 hours until the meringue is crisp. Cool on a wire rack.

Meanwhile, purée half the apricots in a blender or rub through a sieve. Chop the remaining apricots and add to the purée. Stir in the sugar, lemon juice and yogurt.

Spoon the apricot filling into the meringue case and decorate with a little grated chocolate. *Serves 6*
○ *Calories 158 (610)*

Poussins with sultana stuffing

Coffee semolina mousse

150 ml (¼ pint) strong black coffee
10 ml (2 level tsp) powdered gelatine
400 ml (¾ pint) filled milk (see page 116)
50 g (2 oz) semolina
75 g (3 oz) caster sugar
2 egg whites
15 g (½ oz) icing sugar, sifted

Heat the coffee without boiling, then remove from the heat. Add the gelatine and stir until dissolved. In a separate pan heat the milk. Add the semolina, bring to the boil, stirring, and simmer gently for about 10 minutes until the mixture thickens. Remove from the heat and stir in the sugar and the coffee liquid. Cool.

Whisk the egg whites until they hold their shape and fold into the coffee mixture. Turn into a serving dish and leave until lightly set. Serve lightly dusted with icing sugar. *Serves 6*
○ *Calories 155 (606)*

Menu 7 : Sunday Lunch for 6

Curried mushroom salad

Apricot stuffed lamb
Parsnip and carrot purée
Brussels sprouts
Jacket potatoes

Plum fool
Spiced meringue flan

The curried mushrooms can be prepared the day before and stored in an airtight container in the refrigerator until just before serving.

Ask your butcher to bone the leg of lamb and don't forget to soak the dried apricots overnight to make them plump and juicy.

Parsnip and carrot purée is an interesting way of serving root vegetables – cook equal quantities of parsnips and carrots in boiling salted water until tender. Drain and mash to a smooth purée with 25 g (1 oz) Flora and seasoning to taste. Cook the jacket potatoes in the oven with the lamb. Cut each well-scrubbed potato in half, brush with a little sunflower oil and cook for about 1 hour until soft and golden brown.

Prepare both desserts in advance. The plum fool, served in individual glasses, makes a colourful, fresh-tasting cold dessert. The spiced meringue flan is equally good cold or hot, and if you decide on the latter, it can be heated through in the oven while the main course is being eaten.

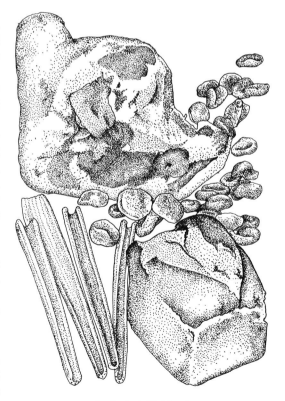

Apricot stuffed lamb

Curried mushroom salad

6 tomatoes, skinned
450 g (1 lb) small button mushrooms, trimmed
100 g (4 oz) lean cooked ham, chopped
1 cucumber, peeled and diced
300 ml (½ pint) low fat natural yogurt
30 ml (2 level tbsp) concentrated curry sauce or 20 ml (4 level tsp) curry powder
salt and freshly ground pepper
20 ml (4 tsp) lemon juice

Cut the tomatoes in half, scoop out the seeds with a teaspoon and chop the flesh. Mix the tomato flesh, mushrooms, ham and cucumber together in a bowl.

Stir the yogurt, curry sauce or powder, seasoning and lemon juice together in a separate bowl. Add the yogurt mixture to the mushroom mixture and stir gently until the vegetables are evenly coated. Chill well in a covered container in the refrigerator before serving. *Serves 6*
○ *Calories 84 (334)*

Apricot stuffed lamb

2-kg (4½-lb) leg of lamb, boned
30 ml (2 level tbsp) flour
300 ml (½ pint) beef stock
salt and freshly ground black pepper

For the stuffing
25 g (1 oz) Flora
4 sticks of celery, washed and finely chopped
1 medium onion, skinned and finely chopped
100 g (4 oz) dried apricots, soaked overnight, drained and finely chopped
100 g (4 oz) fresh brown breadcrumbs
grated rind and juice of ½ lemon
5 ml (1 level tsp) salt
freshly ground black pepper

For the stuffing, melt the margarine in a saucepan and fry the celery and onion for 10 minutes until soft. Remove the pan from the heat, add the remaining ingredients and stir thoroughly until the stuffing is well blended.

Fill the bone cavity of the lamb with the stuffing, pushing it well down. Secure with skewers if the leg has been split open along one side. Place the lamb in a roasting tin, season well and cover with foil. Roast in the oven at 200°C (400°F) mark 6 for 2 hours, basting occasionally with any juices in the pan. Remove the foil 30 minutes before the end of the cooking time so that the skin becomes crisp.

Remove the meat from the roasting tin and keep warm. Drain fat from the roasting tin, leaving about 15 ml (1 tbsp) of meat juices. Add the flour and cook over a low heat until golden brown. Stir in the stock and seasoning and bring to the boil, stirring. Add any meat juices that have separated from the surplus fat. Serve this gravy with the lamb. *Serves 6*
● *Calories 591 (2491)*

Plum fool

450 g (1 lb) fresh plums or 567-g (1 lb 4-oz) can red plums, drained
30 ml (2 level tbsp) sugar
45 ml (3 level tbsp) custard powder
400 ml (¾ pint) filled milk (see page 116)

Cook fresh plums, with just enough water to cover the bottom of the pan, for 5–10 minutes until very tender. Remove the stones and skin from fresh or canned plums, then purée in a blender or rub through a sieve.

Blend the sugar and custard powder together with a little of the measured milk. Heat the remaining milk to boiling point. Pour on to the custard mixture then return to the pan. Bring back to the boil, stirring, and cook for 1 minute. Cover the custard with a piece of dampened greaseproof paper to prevent a skin forming and leave until cool.

Remove the paper from the custard and whip until creamy. Add the plum purée and whip again until well blended. Divide the mixture between individual glasses and chill thoroughly in the refrigerator before serving. *Serves 6*
○ *Calories 176 (714)*

Spiced meringue flan

175 g (6 oz) all-in-one shortcrust pastry (see page 100)

For the filling
25 g (1 oz) Flora
75 g (3 oz) currants
75 g (3 oz) sultanas
25 g (1 oz) chopped mixed peel
50 g (2 oz) soft brown sugar
1·25 ml ($\frac{1}{4}$ level tsp) grated nutmeg
2·5 ml ($\frac{1}{2}$ level tsp) ground cinnamon
2·5 ml ($\frac{1}{2}$ level tsp) mixed spice
grated rind and juice of 1 orange

For the topping
3 egg whites
50 g (2 oz) caster sugar

Spiced meringue flan

Roll out the pastry dough and use to line a 20·5-cm (8-in) flan ring.

For the filling, melt the margarine in a saucepan, add the remaining ingredients and stir until well blended. Spoon into the pastry case. Bake in the oven at 200°C (400°F) mark 6 for about 25 minutes.

Whisk the egg whites until they stand in peaks. Add half the sugar and whisk again until stiff and shiny. Fold in the remaining sugar with a metal spoon or spatula. Spoon the meringue over the flan and return to the oven for 5 minutes until golden brown and crisp. Serve hot or cold. *Serves 6*
◑ *Calories 411 (1717)*

Menu 8 : Dinner Party for 6 *(illustrated in colour facing page 33)*

Devilled mushrooms	Veal escalopes in cider sauce	Tutti frutti pineapple rings
	Boiled rice	
	Broccoli or green beans	

Prepare the Devilled mushrooms in advance and reheat without boiling just before spooning on to the hot toast.

The Tutti frutti pineapple rings can be stored for a few hours in a covered container in the refrigerator.

Devilled mushrooms

25 g (1 oz) Flora
350 g (12 oz) button mushrooms
6 slices of bread
chopped parsley to garnish

For the sauce
120 ml (8 level tbsp) low fat natural yogurt
15 ml (1 tbsp) lemon juice
1·25 ml ($\frac{1}{4}$ tsp) Tabasco sauce
30 ml (2 level tbsp) tomato paste
30 ml (2 level tbsp) horseradish cream
10 ml (2 tsp) Worcestershire sauce
pinch grated nutmeg
salt and freshly ground black pepper

Melt the margarine in a large saucepan, stir in the mushrooms and cook gently for 5 minutes. Beat together the sauce ingredients; stir into the mushrooms. Heat gently for 2 minutes, without boiling.

Cut the crusts from the bread, cut each slice in half and toast under a hot grill. Place the toast on a large heated serving plate and spoon the mushroom mixture on top. Sprinkle with chopped parsley and serve immediately. *Serves 6*
◯ *Calories 141 (568)*

Veal escalopes in cider sauce

6 175-g (6-oz) veal escalopes
25 g (1 oz) Flora
1 medium onion, skinned and thinly sliced
1 large cooking apple, peeled, cored and chopped
2 sticks of celery, washed and sliced
25 g (1 oz) flour
150 ml ($\frac{1}{4}$ pint) chicken stock
150 ml ($\frac{1}{4}$ pint) dry cider
5 ml (1 level tsp) salt
freshly ground black pepper
$\frac{1}{2}$ bunch of watercress to garnish

For the stuffing
75 g (3 oz) dried prunes, soaked overnight
1 large cooking apple, peeled, cored and chopped
1 large onion, skinned and finely chopped
30 ml (2 tbsp) chopped parsley
15 ml (1 tbsp) lemon juice
100 g (4 oz) fresh white breadcrumbs

Trim all visible fat from the meat. Place the escalopes between two sheets of greaseproof paper and flatten with a meat hammer or rolling pin. For the stuffing, stir all the ingredients together in a bowl. Spread over the escalopes, roll up and secure with wooden cocktail sticks or string.

Melt the margarine in a large frying pan and fry the escalope rolls for about 10 minutes until golden brown on all sides. Remove from the pan and reserve. Add the onion, apple and celery to the pan and fry for 5 minutes. Stir in the flour, cook for 1 minute and gradually stir in the stock, cider and seasoning. Bring to the boil, stirring, and cook for 2 minutes. Return the escalope rolls to the pan, cover and simmer gently for 45–50 minutes until the veal is tender. Serve the escalopes and sauce on a bed of rice, garnished with watercress. *Serves 6*
◗ *Calories 335 (1366)*

Tutti frutti pineapple rings

1 ripe pineapple
225 g (8 oz) curd cheese
30 ml (2 tbsp) Kirsch
50 g (2 oz) caster sugar
25 g (1 oz) glacé cherries
25 g (1 oz) walnuts, finely chopped
10 ml (2 level tsp) finely chopped angelica

For the syrup
30 ml (2 level tbsp) sugar
150 ml ($\frac{1}{4}$ pint) water
15 ml (1 tbsp) Kirsch

Cut the top and bottom from the pineapple, then cut away the skin. Cut into six thick slices and remove the hard centre core. Place the pineapple in one layer on a shallow serving dish.

For the syrup, place the sugar and water in a small saucepan and heat gently until the sugar has dissolved. Boil rapidly until reduced by half. Cool, then add the Kirsch and pour the syrup over the pineapple. Cover and chill for 30 minutes.

Meanwhile, place the cheese in a bowl

and beat until smooth. Stir in the Kirsch and sugar. Reserve three cherries for decoration and finely chop the rest. Add to the cheese with the nuts and angelica. Spoon the cheese filling into a piping bag fitted with a large rosette nozzle. Pipe the filling over the centre of each pineapple ring and top with the halved reserved cherries. *Serves 6*
○ *Calories 196 (777)*

Menu 9 : Chinese Dinner Party for 6

Beef and tomato soup	*Chicken with ham and almonds*	*Chinese fruit salad*
	Veal with bamboo shoots	
	Fried rice with mushrooms and bean	
	sprouts	
	Stir-fried Chinese leaves with orange	

Prepare the Chinese fruit salad and leave in the refrigerator to chill thoroughly.

Almost all Chinese food has to be cooked at the last minute, but the ingredients should be prepared in advance in the true Chinese manner. Peel, cut and chop the vegetables, fruits and meats, cover and keep in the refrigerator until ready to cook. The rice for the Fried rice with mushrooms and bean sprouts should be cooked beforehand.

Follow the recipes for the four main course dishes, but rather than keeping the food warm in the oven, leave in the various pans and reheat quickly over a high heat just before serving.

Beef and tomato soup

225-g (8-oz) piece rump steak
15 ml (1 level tbsp) cornflour
5 ml (1 level tsp) salt
freshly ground black pepper
1·8 litres (3 pints) beef stock
bunch of spring onions, trimmed and chopped
4 medium tomatoes, skinned and chopped
bouquet garni
2·5 ml ($\frac{1}{2}$ level tsp) sugar
chopped fresh chives to garnish

Trim any visible fat from the steak and cut into 2·5-cm (1-in) strips. Stir the cornflour and seasoning together and use to coat the beef. Bring the stock to the boil in a large saucepan and add the strips of beef, spring onions, tomatoes and bouquet garni. Simmer for 5 minutes. Add the sugar and simmer for a further 2–3 minutes. Remove the bouquet garni and serve sprinkled with chopped fresh chives. *Serves 6*
◗ *Calories 97 (401)*

Chicken with ham and almonds

450 g (1 lb) chicken breasts, skinned
15 ml (1 tbsp) vegetable oil
1 large onion, skinned and chopped
2 slices of root ginger, peeled and finely chopped *or* 5 ml (1 level tsp) ground ginger
1 small red pepper, seeded and thinly sliced
100 g (4 oz) lean cooked ham, diced
25 g (1 oz) Flora
15 ml (1 level tbsp) cornflour
300 ml ($\frac{1}{2}$ pint) chicken stock
5 ml (1 level tsp) salt
freshly ground black pepper
$\frac{1}{2}$ cucumber, diced
25 g (1 oz) whole almonds, toasted

Remove any bone from the chicken breasts and cut into thin strips. Heat the oil in a large frying pan, add the chicken and onion and fry for 5 minutes stirring. Add the ginger, red pepper and ham and cook for a further 5 minutes, stirring. Remove from the pan and keep warm.

Main course fish chowder *(page 60)* ▶

Add the margarine to the pan, stir in the cornflour and cook for 1 minute. Gradually stir in the stock and bring to the boil. Add the seasoning, cucumber and almonds and simmer for 2 minutes. Return the chicken mixture to the pan and cook for a further 5 minutes to heat through. *Serves 6*
◖ *Calories 231 (898)*

Veal with bamboo shoots

700 g (1½ lb) lean veal
15 ml (1 tbsp) sunflower oil
1 onion, skinned and chopped
100 g (4 oz) carrot, peeled and cut into
   matchsticks
141-g (5-oz) can bamboo shoots, drained and
   sliced
60 ml (4 tbsp) soy sauce
60 ml (4 tbsp) dry sherry
5 ml (1 level tsp) sugar
10 ml (2 level tsp) cornflour
120 ml (8 tbsp) water
113-g (4-oz) packet frozen peas
5 ml (1 level tsp) salt
freshly ground black pepper

Trim any visible fat from the veal and cut into 1-cm (½-in) dice. Heat the oil in a large frying pan, add the veal and onion and cook for 15 minutes, stirring. Add the carrot and bamboo shoots. Cook for another 6 minutes. Stir in the soy sauce, sherry and sugar.

Mix the cornflour to a smooth paste with the water and add to the pan. Bring to the boil and simmer gently for 2 minutes until thickened. Add the peas and seasoning and cook for 5 minutes longer until the peas are tender. *Serves 6*
◖ *Calories 182 (760)*

Fried rice with mushrooms and bean sprouts

450 g (1 lb) long grain rice
30 ml (2 tbsp) sunflower oil
4 spring onions, trimmed and finely chopped
1 clove of garlic, skinned and crushed
1 green pepper, seeded and sliced
225 g (8 oz) button mushrooms, sliced
275 g (10 oz) fresh bean sprouts
15 ml (1 tbsp) soy sauce
5 ml (1 level tsp) salt
freshly ground black pepper

Cook the rice in boiling salted water for 12 minutes and drain. Heat the oil in a large frying pan, add the onions and garlic and fry for 2 minutes. Add the pepper and mushrooms and cook for 2–3 minutes, stirring. Stir in the rice and bean sprouts and cook for another 3–4 minutes. Add the soy sauce and seasoning and stir over the heat for another minute before serving. *Serves 6*
○ *Calories 155 (643)*

Stir-fried Chinese leaves with orange

15 ml (1 tbsp) sunflower oil
25 g (1 oz) Flora
1 clove of garlic, skinned and crushed
2 large heads of Chinese leaves, finely
   shredded
grated rind and juice of 1 large orange
10 ml (2 tsp) soy sauce
10 ml (2 level tsp) sugar
30 ml (2 tbsp) dry sherry

Heat the oil and margarine in a large frying pan and fry the garlic and Chinese leaves

◀ Haddock paprika *(page 65)*

over a high heat for 2 minutes, stirring continuously. Add the remaining ingredients and cook over a low heat for a further 2 minutes, stirring. *Serves 6*
○ *Calories 68 (263)*

Chinese fruit salad

1 small watermelon
1 small honeydew melon, halved and seeded
1 small fresh pineapple
425-g (15-oz) can guavas
2 oranges, peeled and segmented
100 g (4 oz) black grapes, halved
2 medium bananas, thinly sliced
5 ml (1 tsp) fresh lemon juice

Cut the watermelon into quarters, remove the seeds and cut the flesh into 1-cm ($\frac{1}{2}$-in) cubes. Cut the flesh of the honeydew melon into balls with a melon baller. Cut the skin from the pineapple. Slice the flesh, remove the centre core from each slice and cut into chunks. Drain the guavas, reserving the juice, and cut into slices.

Place the prepared fruits in a large glass serving dish with any juice. Add the juice from the guavas and lemon juice and stir well. Serve chilled. *Serves 6*
○ *Calories 132 (539)*

Menu 10 : Buffet for 10

Grapefruit salad
Potted beef

Bacon stuffed turkey
Pepper salad
Courgette and mushroom salad
Italian pasta salad

Blackberry and almond meringue
Chocolate hazelnut creams

The buffet party is often planned as part of a family celebration of some kind, whether a birthday, wedding, christening or anniversary. This selection of food will appeal to all age groups, whether following a cholesterol-lowering diet or not.

The dishes have been chosen because they can all be prepared one or two days before the buffet, giving you plenty of time to arrange the room and set the table on the day. Two starters, one refreshing and one more solid, cater for varying appetites. Turkey is a good buy for a crowd and is available all the year round. And a party isn't a party without a sumptuous dessert: here are two that can be enjoyed by everyone without harmful after effects.

This buffet is planned to feed ten people but you can multiply or divide the quantities to provide a spread for a smaller or larger group.

Grapefruit salad

3 medium yellow grapefruit
2 medium pink grapefruit
5 satsumas, peeled and segmented
225 g (8 oz) black grapes, skinned, halved and seeded
225 g (8 oz) white grapes, skinned, halved and seeded
30 ml (2 tbsp) chopped fresh mint
60 ml (4 level tbsp) caster sugar
mint sprigs to garnish

Cut the grapefruit in half and cut out the segments with a grapefruit knife. Place in a bowl with any juice. Remove the membrane from the grapefruit shells. Add the satsumas, grapes, mint and sugar to the grapefruit. Mix well, cover and chill overnight. Spoon the fruit into the reserved grapefruit shells and garnish with sprigs of mint. *Serves 10*
○ *Calories 79 (322)*

Potted beef

900 g (2 lb) chuck steak
300 ml ($\frac{1}{2}$ pint) beef stock
2 cloves of garlic, skinned and crushed
2 blades of mace
salt and freshly ground black pepper
100 g (4 oz) Flora
fresh bay leaves to garnish
Melba toast

Trim any visible fat from the beef and cut into 1-cm ($\frac{1}{2}$-in) cubes. Place in an oven-proof casserole with the stock, garlic, mace and seasoning. Cover and cook in the oven at 180°C (350°F) mark 4 for $2\frac{1}{2}$ hours until tender. Remove the mace, drain off the stock and reserve.

Mince the meat twice until smooth. Melt 25 g (1 oz) of the margarine and add to the meat with enough stock to moisten it. Press into ten 150-ml ($\frac{1}{4}$-pint) soufflé dishes and pour over the remaining margarine, melted. Chill overnight. Garnish with bay leaves and serve with Melba toast. *Serves 10*
⬤ *Calories 251 (1003)*

Bacon stuffed turkey

4·5-kg (10-lb) oven-ready turkey, boned
15 ml (1 tbsp) sunflower oil
tomato wedges and watercress to garnish

For the stuffing
75 g (3 oz) Flora
225 g (8 oz) onion, skinned and chopped
6 sticks of celery, washed and chopped
450 g (1 lb) lean bacon, rinded and finely
    chopped
salt and freshly ground black pepper
350 g (12 oz) fresh white breadcrumbs
350 g (12 oz) mushrooms, chopped
75 g (3 oz) toasted almonds, chopped
grated rind and juice of 3 lemons

For the stuffing, melt the margarine in a large saucepan, add the onion, celery and bacon and fry gently for 15 minutes. Stir in the seasoning, breadcrumbs, mushrooms, almonds, lemon rind and lemon juice. Mix well.

Lay the boned turkey out flat, skin side down. Spoon the stuffing down the centre. Fold over the two ends then the sides to enclose the stuffing. Sew up with string and a trussing needle. Turn the turkey over, weigh it, brush with the oil and wrap in foil. Place in a roasting tin and cook in the oven at 180°C (350°F) mark 4 for 15 minutes per 450 g (1 lb) plus 15 minutes. Unwrap the turkey for the last 30 minutes to brown the skin. Leave to cool and then chill overnight. Slice the turkey and arrange on a large serving dish, garnished with tomato wedges and watercress. *Serves 10–12*
⬤ *Calories 501 (2115)*

Pepper salad

2 large yellow peppers, seeded and sliced
3 large red peppers, seeded and sliced
2 large green peppers, seeded and sliced
2 medium onions, skinned and sliced
chopped parsley to garnish

For the dressing
60 ml (4 tbsp) wine vinegar
120 ml (8 tbsp) sunflower oil
5 ml (1 level tsp) made mustard
salt and freshly ground black pepper
2 cloves of garlic, skinned and crushed

Blanch the peppers and onions in boiling salted water for 2 minutes. Drain. Plunge into cold water and drain again. Place in a large mixing bowl.

Whisk together the dressing ingredients and pour over the salad. Toss well until evenly coated, cover and chill overnight. Spoon into a serving dish and sprinkle with parsley. *Serves 10*
○ *Calories 134 (555)*

Courgette and mushroom salad

25 g (1 oz) Flora
1·4 kg (3 lb) courgettes, trimmed and sliced
grated rind and juice of 2 lemons
350 g (12 oz) button mushrooms, sliced

For the dressing
60 ml (4 tbsp) wine vinegar
120 ml (8 tbsp) sunflower oil
5 ml (1 level tsp) made mustard
salt and freshly ground black pepper

Melt the margarine in a large frying pan, add the courgettes and fry for 5–6 minutes until just tender and a light golden brown. Place in a large mixing bowl, add the lemon rind and pour over the juice. Whisk the dressing ingredients together in a small bowl and pour over the courgettes. Stir in the mushrooms, toss well, cover and chill overnight. Spoon into a serving dish.
Serves 10
○ *Calories 42 (167)*

Italian pasta salad

350 g (12 oz) small pasta shells
2 cucumbers, diced
20 black olives, halved and stoned
450 g (1 lb) tomatoes, skinned, seeded and
    chopped
1 bunch radishes, trimmed, washed and sliced
60 ml (4 tbsp) chopped parsley

For the dressing
60 ml (4 tbsp) wine vinegar
120 ml (8 tbsp) sunflower oil
5 ml (1 level tsp) made mustard
salt and freshly ground black pepper

Cook the pasta in a pan of boiling salted water for 15 minutes and drain well. Whisk the dressing ingredients together, pour over the pasta and toss well until evenly coated. Leave to cool.

Stir in the cucumber, olives, tomatoes, radishes and parsley. Cover and chill overnight. Spoon the salad into a serving dish.
Serves 10
○ *Calories 168 (702)*

Blackberry and almond meringue

Instead of spreading the meringue, it may be piped on to the flan using a large vegetable nozzle.

350 g (12 oz) all-in-one shortcrust pastry (see
    page 100)
900 g (2 lb) blackberries, washed
450 g (1 lb) cooking apples, peeled, cored and
    thinly sliced
120 ml (8 tbsp) water
50 g (2 oz) caster sugar
50 g (2 oz) ground almonds
5 ml (1 tsp) almond essence

For the meringue
6 egg whites
100 g (4 oz) caster sugar

Roll out the pastry dough and use to line two 20·5-cm (8-in) flan rings.

Place the blackberries and apple in a saucepan with the water. Cover the fruit

Blackberry and almond meringue

and simmer for 8–10 minutes until just tender. Stir in the sugar, ground almonds and almond essence and pour into the pastry cases. Bake in the oven at 190°C (375°F) mark 5 for 15 minutes.

Whisk the egg whites until they stand in peaks. Whisk in half the sugar until smooth and shiny. Fold in the remaining sugar with a metal spoon or spatula and spoon the meringue over the flans. Spread to the edges and pull into peaks with the back of a spoon. Return to the oven at 180°C (350°F) mark 4 and bake for 20 minutes until golden brown and crisp. These flans may either be served cold or reheated in the oven at 180°C (350°F) mark 4 for 15 minutes.
Serves 10–12
◑ *Calories 391 (1534)*

Chocolate hazelnut creams

450 g (1 lb) curd cheese
25 g (1 oz) cocoa powder
60 ml (4 tbsp) warm skimmed milk
100 g (4 oz) caster sugar
300 ml ($\frac{1}{2}$ pint) low fat hazelnut yogurt
4 egg whites
chopped toasted hazelnuts to garnish

Place the cheese in a mixing bowl and beat for a few minutes until smooth. Blend the cocoa into the warm milk and beat into the cheese. Stir in the sugar and yogurt. Whisk the egg whites until stiff and fold into the cheese mixture. Spoon into ten individual glass dishes and chill overnight. Sprinkle with the chopped nuts before serving.
Serves 10
○ *Calories 163 (660)*

Menu 11 : Children's Party for 12

Pinwheel and Chequerboard sandwiches	*Cheese and Marmite straws*	*Peach and jelly crisp*
Quiche tartlets	*Savoury choux puffs*	*Butterscotch bars*

Do as much preparation as possible well in advance of the party; you will need all your wits and energy for things other than food!

The sandwiches can be cut the evening before, as long as they are closely covered with foil or cling film and kept overnight in the refrigerator. Remove them an hour or so before tea time. Similarly, the little quiches, the Cheese and Marmite straws and the Butterscotch bars can be completed the day before the party.

Only the filling of the choux puffs and the topping for the jelly need be left until the morning of the party – they will go soggy if prepared too far in advance.

Finally, provide plenty to drink – fruit juices and squashes are ideal, or milk shakes, made with skimmed milk if necessary.

Pinwheel and Chequerboard sandwiches

Pinwheels
Cut a large tin loaf lengthways into thin slices and remove the crusts. Spread each slice with sandwich filling, right to the edges, and roll up like a Swiss roll from the short edge. Wrap in kitchen foil and store in the refrigerator until firm. Just before serving cut across into pinwheels.

Chequerboards
Spread slices of brown bread with filling and top with slices of white bread. Cut each sandwich into 4 small square sandwiches. Arrange alternately, brown or white bread uppermost, to form a chequerboard.

Sandwich fillings

25 g (1 oz) Flora
1 medium banana, mashed
lemon juice

Beat the ingredients together until well blended.
○ *Calories 268 (1126), whole recipe*

25 g (1 oz) Flora
120 g (4½ oz) can pilchards in tomato sauce

Beat the ingredients together until well blended.
◑ *Calories 449 (1886), whole recipe*

25 g (1 oz) Flora
100 g (4 oz) cottage cheese, sieved
1 small orange, peeled and finely chopped

Beat the ingredients together until well blended.
○ *Calories 343 (1441), whole recipe*

25 g (1 oz) Flora
Marmite to taste
50 g (2 oz) Edam cheese, finely grated

Beat the ingredients together until well blended.
◑ *Calories 335 (1407), whole recipe*

Quiche tartlets

100 g (4 oz) all-in-one shortcrust pastry (see
   page 100)
75 g (3 oz) Edam cheese, grated
150 ml (¼ pint) skimmed milk
1 egg
1·25 ml (¼ level tsp) dried mixed herbs
salt and freshly ground black pepper
tomato slices and sprigs of parsley to garnish

Roll out the pastry dough and use to line 12–14 patty tins. Divide the grated cheese between the pastry cases. Lightly whisk together the milk, egg and herbs. Season to taste and spoon into the pastry cases. Bake in the oven at 180°C (350°F) mark 4 for 20–25 minutes. Garnish with slices of tomato and sprigs of parsley. *Makes 12–14*
◑ *Calories 102 (428)*

Cheese and Marmite straws

100 g (4 oz) plain flour
salt and freshly ground black pepper
50 g (2 oz) Flora
50 g (2 oz) Edam cheese, grated
cold water to mix
Marmite

Sift the flour with the salt and pepper and rub in the margarine until the mixture resembles fine breadcrumbs. Stir in the cheese and enough cold water to mix to a stiff dough. Roll out the dough thinly and trim into oblongs 20 × 7 cm (8 × 2½ in). Spread the dough oblongs thinly with Marmite and cut into straws. Twist the straws and place on a greased baking sheet.

Roll out the remaining pastry scraps and cut into rounds with a 5-cm (2-in) plain cutter. Cut out the centre of the rounds with a 3-cm (1½-in) plain cutter to make rings. Bake in the oven at 200°C (400°F) mark 6 for 10–15 minutes. Cool and use the rings to hold together a small bundle of straws to serve.
◑ *Calories 955 (4011), whole recipe*

Savoury choux puffs

150 ml (¼ pint) water
50 g (2 oz) Flora
65 g (2½ oz) flour, sifted
2 eggs, beaten

For the filling
210-g (7½-oz) can pilchards, mashed
juice of ½ lemon
30 ml (2 level tbsp) cottage cheese, sieved
paprika to sprinkle

Place the water and margarine in a saucepan. Heat gently until the margarine has melted, then bring to boil. Remove from the heat and beat in the flour with a wooden spoon for 1–2 minutes until the mixture leaves the sides of pan. Cool slightly.

Gradually add the beaten eggs, beating well between each addition. Using 2 teaspoons place small balls of mixture well apart on greased baking sheets. Bake in the oven at 220°C (425°F) mark 7 for 15–20 minutes until well risen and golden brown. Cool on a wire rack.

Mash the filling ingredients together until well blended. Make a slit in the side of each puff and spoon or pipe in the filling. Sprinkle with paprika. *Makes 16–20*
⬤ *Calories 1072 (4502), whole recipe*

Peach and jelly crisp

1½ tangerine jelly tablets
900 ml (1½ pints) boiling water
2 425-g (15-oz) cans peaches, drained
400 ml (¾ pint) low fat natural yogurt
75 g (3 oz) Flora
45 ml (3 level tbsp) golden syrup
175 g (6 oz) cornflakes

Break up the jelly, pour over the boiling water and stir until dissolved. Add the peaches and leave in a cold place to set. Just before the jelly sets swirl in the yogurt but do not overmix. Turn the mixture into a serving dish.

Stir the margarine and syrup in a pan over a gentle heat until melted, then stir in the cornflakes. Spoon on top of the jelly and press down gently. Leave to set thoroughly.
◯ *Calories 210 (865)*

Butterscotch bars

75 g (3 oz) Flora
75 g (3 oz) golden syrup
100 g (4 oz) stoned dates, chopped, or seedless raisins
50 g (2 oz) glacé cherries, chopped
50 g (2 oz) walnuts, chopped
100 g (4 oz) wheatmeal biscuits, crumbled

Heat the margarine and golden syrup in a saucepan. Bring to the boil, stirring continuously, and boil for 2–3 minutes. Set aside.

Mix together the remaining ingredients, pour over the syrup mixture and stir until coated evenly. Press into an 18-cm (7-in) square cake tin. Chill in the refrigerator until set and cut into 12 bars for serving. *Makes 12*
◗ *Calories 179 (752) per bar*

Recipe Section

Soups and starters
Fish
Meat and poultry
Vegetables and salads
Puddings and desserts
Baking
Snacks and savouries
Sauces and dressings
Dairy food substitutes
Useful tables

Soups and Starters

Beefy onion soup

25 g (1 oz) Flora
350 g (12 oz) onions, skinned and sliced
900 ml (1½ pints) beef stock
5 ml (1 level tsp) Marmite or Bovril
1·25 ml (¼ level tsp) dried thyme
bay leaf
salt and freshly ground black pepper

Melt the margarine in a large saucepan and fry the onions for 12–15 minutes until brown. Add the remaining ingredients, bring to the boil and simmer for 20 minutes. Serve hot with croûtons fried in Flora or baked in the oven without fat.
○ *Calories 82 (323)*

Farmhouse chicken soup

25 g (1 oz) Flora
2 carrots, peeled and diced
2 sticks celery, washed and chopped
1 onion, skinned and chopped
225 g (8 oz) chicken meat, cubed
900 ml (1½ pints) water
chicken carcass, or chicken stock cubes
salt and freshly ground black pepper

Melt the margarine in large pan and fry the vegetables gently for 5 minutes. Add the chicken and water with the carcass or stock cubes and seasoning. Bring to the boil, reduce the heat and simmer for 2 hours.

Strain the soup and discard the bones, if used. Purée the soup in a blender or rub through a sieve. Adjust the seasoning and serve with croûtons fried in Flora or baked in the oven without fat.
◑ *Calories 175 (718) plus about 60 (250) with fried croûtons*

Cauliflower soup

25 g (1 oz) Flora
1 large cauliflower, washed and broken into florets
1 onion, skinned and chopped
600 ml (1 pint) beef stock
300 ml (½ pint) filled milk (see page 116)
salt and freshly ground black pepper
chopped parsley to garnish

Melt the margarine in a large saucepan and fry the cauliflower and onion gently for 5 minutes until softened. Add the stock and filled milk and the seasoning. Bring to the boil and simmer for 25–30 minutes until the vegetables are quite tender. Purée in a

blender or rub through a sieve. Adjust the seasoning and serve garnished with chopped parsley.
○ *Calories 164 (664)*

Hearty winter broth

50 g (2 oz) Flora
1 large onion, skinned and chopped
3 carrots, peeled and diced
1 leek, sliced and washed
2 sticks celery, washed and finely chopped
1 small swede, peeled and diced
50 g (2 oz) split brown lentils
1·2 litres (2 pints) beef stock
salt and freshly ground black pepper
chopped parsley to garnish

Melt the margarine in a large saucepan, add the vegetables and fry for 3–5 minutes without allowing them to brown. Add the

lentils, stock and seasoning. Bring to the boil and simmer gently for 45 minutes to 1 hour. Adjust the seasoning and serve hot, sprinkled with parsley.
○ *Calories 201 (764)*

Tomato and onion soup

25 g (1 oz) Flora
1 clove of garlic, skinned and crushed
2 large onions, skinned and chopped
700 g (1½ lb) tomatoes, skinned and chopped
1–2 carrots, peeled and sliced
25 g (1 oz) bran
1·2 litres (2 pints) chicken stock
5 ml (1 level tsp) sugar
2·5 ml (½ level tsp) dried basil
salt and freshly ground black pepper
30 ml (2 tbsp) low fat natural yogurt

Melt the margarine in a large saucepan and

Hearty winter broth

fry the garlic and onions gently for 5 minutes until softened. Add the tomatoes and carrots and cook gently for 1–2 minutes. Stir in the bran and stock and add the sugar, basil and seasoning. Bring to the boil and simmer for 30 minutes. Purée in a blender or rub through a sieve. Adjust the seasoning, reheat and serve with a swirl of yogurt on each bowl. *Serves 4–6*
○ *Calories 132 (529) for 4*
90 (353) for 6

Carrot and onion soup

25 g (1 oz) Flora
450 g (1 lb) carrots, peeled and thinly sliced
2 onions, skinned and chopped
1 clove of garlic, skinned and crushed
750 ml (1¼ pints) beef stock
salt and freshly ground black pepper
30 ml (2 tbsp) low fat natural yogurt
chopped parsley or grated nutmeg to garnish

Melt the margarine in a large saucepan. Fry the vegetables and garlic for 5 minutes. Add the stock and seasoning, bring to the boil and simmer for 15–20 minutes until the carrots are tender. Purée the soup in a blender or rub through a sieve. Adjust the seasoning and reheat. Add a swirl of yogurt and some parsley or nutmeg to each serving.
○ *Calories 102 (410)*

Bavarian leek soup

25 g (1 oz) Flora
1 small onion, skinned and finely chopped
2 small leeks, washed and chopped
25 g (1 oz) plain flour
300 ml (½ pint) skimmed milk
2 chicken stock cubes
900 ml (1½ pints) water
50 g (2 oz) lean cooked ham, sliced into thin strips
salt and freshly ground black pepper

Melt the margarine in a large saucepan and gently fry the onion and leeks for 5 minutes until softened. Stir in the flour and cook for

1 minute. Gradually stir in the milk and stock made from the stock cubes and water. Bring to the boil and simmer for 45–50 minutes. Add the ham and continue cooking gently for another 5 minutes. Season with salt and pepper to taste. *Serves 4–6*
◖ *Calories 151 (588) for 4*
100 (391) for 6

Main course fish chowder

Illustrated in colour facing page 48

450 g (1 lb) haddock fillets, skinned and cut into bite-size pieces
1 leek, sliced and washed
1 onion, skinned and chopped
4 tomatoes, skinned and quartered
1 potato, peeled and sliced
salt and freshly ground black pepper
bouquet garni
400 ml (¾ pint) cider
400 ml (¾ pint) water
1 small French loaf, sliced
50 g (2 oz) Flora
50 g (2 oz) Edam cheese, grated
chopped parsley to garnish

Place the fish in a large saucepan with the leek, onion, tomatoes and potato. Season well, add the bouquet garni and cover with the cider and water. Simmer gently for 30 minutes.
    Spread the sliced bread with margarine and sprinkle each slice with grated cheese. Pour the soup into an ovenproof tureen and top with the slices of bread. Place in the oven at 200°C (400°F) mark 6 until the soup is hot and the cheese bubbles.
◖ *Calories 457 (1844)*

Smoked mackerel pâté

1 medium smoked mackerel, skinned and filleted
150 g (5 oz) Flora
juice of 2 lemons
1 clove of garlic, skinned and crushed
freshly ground black pepper

Flake the mackerel into a large bowl and

add the margarine, lemon juice and crushed garlic. Work the ingredients to a paste with a wooden spoon and season to taste with black pepper. Press the pâté into individual ramekin dishes and chill thoroughly. Serve with toast or biscuits.

◗ *Calories 400 (1760)*

Aubergine hors d'oeuvre

2 large aubergines, peeled and roughly
  chopped
50 g (2 oz) Flora
1 onion, skinned and chopped
2 tomatoes, skinned and sliced
60 ml (4 tbsp) wine vinegar
25 g (1 oz) sugar
5 ml (1 level tsp) dried oregano
15 ml (1 level tbsp) capers
6–8 black olives, halved and stoned
1 small lettuce, washed

Sprinkle the aubergine flesh with salt and allow to drain in a colander for 30 minutes. Rinse with cold water and dry on kitchen paper towel. Melt the margarine in a frying pan and fry the onion and aubergine for 5 minutes until softened. Add the tomatoes, vinegar, sugar and oregano and simmer gently for 10–15 minutes until tender. Add the capers and halved olives. Remove from the heat and allow to cool. Serve with lettuce leaves on individual plates as a starter or side salad.

○ *Calories 165 (567)*

Courgettes au gratin

25 g (1 oz) Flora
4 large courgettes, sliced diagonally
4 tomatoes, skinned and sliced
175 g (6 oz) mushrooms, sliced
grated rind and juice of 1 lemon
300 ml ($\frac{1}{2}$ pint) all-in-one coating cheese
  sauce (see page 114)
25 g (1 oz) Edam cheese, grated
25 g (1 oz) fresh white breadcrumbs

Melt the margarine in a saucepan and gently fry the courgettes, tomatoes and mushrooms for 3–5 minutes with the lemon rind and juice. Turn into an oven-proof dish. Pour over the cheese sauce and sprinkle the top with the grated cheese and breadcrumbs. Bake in the oven at 200°C (400°F) mark 6 for 30–40 minutes until golden brown and bubbling.

◗ *Calories 259 (1042)*

Provençale flan

225 g (8 oz) all-in-one wholemeal pastry (see
  page 100)

For the filling
50 g (2 oz) Flora
4 tomatoes, skinned and quartered
30 ml (2 level tbsp) tomato paste
3 large onions, skinned and chopped
1 clove of garlic, skinned and crushed
25 g (1 oz) anchovy fillets, drained
6 stuffed olives, sliced

Roll out the pastry dough and use to line a 20·5-cm (8-in) flan case. Bake blind in the oven at 220°C (425°F) mark 7 for 10 minutes

For the filling, melt half the margarine in a saucepan, add the tomatoes and tomato paste and simmer gently until the mixture becomes a thick purée. Melt the remaining margarine and fry the onions and garlic for 5–10 minutes until soft and golden. Cover the bottom of the cooled flan case with the tomato mixture, then cover with the onions. Arrange the anchovy fillets and olives on top. Bake in the oven at 180°C (350°F) mark 4 for 30 minutes. Serve hot or cold, cut in slices. *Serves 6*

○ *Calories 463 (1806)*

Chicken melon bowl

1 large honeydew melon, halved and seeded
225 g (8 oz) cooked chicken, cut into cubes
1 green pepper, seeded and diced
50 g (2 oz) walnuts, roughly chopped
30–45 ml (2–3 tbsp) low fat natural yogurt
5 ml (1 level tsp) paprika

Scoop out the melon flesh with a melon

baller or teaspoon. Place the melon in a large bowl, add all the remaining ingredients and toss together gently until well mixed. Pile the mixture back into the melon halves to serve.

◗ *Calories 268 (1100)*

Seafood cocktail

65-g (2½-oz) can salmon, drained and flaked
2 sticks celery, washed and finely chopped
lettuce leaves, shredded
4 lemon slices to garnish

For the dressing
15 ml (1 level tbsp) tomato paste
15 ml (1 tbsp) lemon juice
5 ml (1 tsp) Worcestershire sauce
30 ml (2 tbsp) low fat natural yogurt
salt and freshly ground pepper

Mix together the salmon and celery. Whisk the dressing ingredients together in a small bowl. Spoon the cocktail on to a base of shredded lettuce in individual glass dishes and coat with the dressing. Garnish with the lemon slices and serve with brown bread spread with Flora.

◗ *Calories 49 (206)*

Mushrooms à la grecque

15 g (½ oz) Flora
1 onion, skinned and sliced
1 clove of garlic, skinned and crushed
450 g (1 lb) button mushrooms
425-g (15-oz) can tomatoes
juice of 1 lemon
bay leaf
6 parsley sprigs
1·25 ml (¼ level tsp) dried basil or thyme
300 ml (½ pint) dry white wine
2·5 ml (½ level tsp) sugar
salt and freshly ground pepper
15 ml (1 level tbsp) cornflour
chopped parsley to garnish

Melt the margarine in a frying pan and fry the onion and garlic for 5 minutes until soft. Add the remaining ingredients except the cornflour and simmer gently for 10–15 minutes.

Blend the cornflour with a little water and add to the mushroom mixture. Stir over a gentle heat until thickened. Serve the mushrooms hot or cold, sprinkled with the chopped parsley and accompanied by French bread.

○ *Calories 122 (500)*

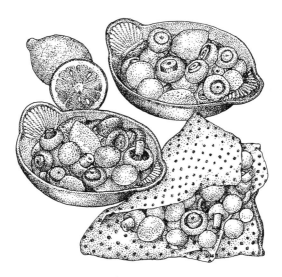

Mushrooms à la grecque

Fish

Eastern spiced fish with rice

175 g (6 oz) long grain rice
50 g (2 oz) sultanas
1 cooking apple, peeled, cored and chopped
15 ml (1 tbsp) sunflower oil
25 g (1 oz) Flora
1 large onion, skinned and chopped
1 clove of garlic, skinned and crushed
2·5 ml (½ level tsp) ground cumin
2·5 ml (½ level tsp) ground coriander
1·25 ml (¼ level tsp) turmeric
1·25 ml (¼ level tsp) ground ginger
pinch chilli powder
700 g (1½ lb) haddock or whiting fillet, skinned
25 g (1 oz) flour
salt and freshly ground black pepper
100 g (4 oz) button mushrooms
150 ml (¼ pint) fish or chicken stock
5 ml (1 tsp) lemon juice
2 tomatoes, skinned, seeded and quartered

Cook the rice in boiling salted water for 10 minutes. Add the sultanas and apple and continue cooking for 2 minutes. Drain, arrange round the edge of a heated serving dish and keep warm.

Meanwhile heat the oil and margarine in a large frying pan, add the onion, garlic and spices and fry for 5 minutes. Cut the fish into 2·5-cm (1-in) cubes and toss in seasoned flour. Add to the pan and cook for 5 minutes, stirring occasionally. Add the mushrooms and cook for a further 2 minutes. Stir in the stock, lemon juice and tomato quarters. Bring to the boil, stirring, and simmer gently for about 5 minutes until the sauce has thickened. Spoon the fish into the rice ring and serve immediately.
○ *Calories 343 (1375)*

Savoury cod and pasta bake

175 g (6 oz) pasta shells
700 g (1½ lb) cod fillet, skinned
15 g (½ oz) Flora
15 g (½ oz) flour
300 ml (½ pint) skimmed milk
15 ml (1 level tbsp) tomato paste
grated rind and juice of 1 lemon
2·5 ml (½ level tsp) dried oregano
30 ml (2 tbsp) chopped parsley
5 ml (1 level tsp) salt
2·5 ml (½ level tsp) paprika
4 ripe tomatoes, skinned and sliced
75 g (3 oz) Edam cheese, grated

Cook the pasta in boiling salted water for 10–12 minutes, then drain. Cut the cod into 2·5-cm (1-in) cubes. Melt the margarine in a saucepan, add the flour and cook for 1 minute. Gradually add the milk and bring to the boil, stirring continuously. Add the tomato paste, lemon rind and juice, oregano, parsley and seasoning, then stir in the fish.

Reserve four slices of tomato for garnish. Arrange the remaining tomato slices, pasta and fish mixture in layers in a greased ovenproof dish, finishing with a layer of pasta on top. Sprinkle with the grated cheese and arrange the reserved tomato slices down the centre. Cook in the oven at 190°C (375°F) mark 5 for 25–30 minutes until golden brown.

Serve with Green pepper and cucumber salad (see page 90).

◗ *Calories 326 (1345)*

Marinated fish kebabs

700 g (1½ lb) cod fillet, skinned
1 corn on the cob
1 small red pepper, seeded
4 small tomatoes, halved
100 g (4 oz) flat mushrooms
225 g (8 oz) long grain rice
1·25 ml (¼ level tsp) turmeric

For the marinade
60 ml (4 tbsp) sunflower oil
30 ml (2 tbsp) red wine vinegar
5 ml (1 level tsp) dried thyme
5 ml (1 level tsp) salt
freshly ground black pepper
30 ml (2 tbsp) lemon juice
1 small onion, skinned and finely chopped

Stir the marinade ingredients together in a large bowl. Cut the fish into 2·5-cm (1-in) cubes. Add to the bowl and stir gently until evenly coated. Cover and leave in a cool place for about 30 minutes.

Blanch the sweetcorn in boiling water for 5 minutes. Plunge into cold water, drain and cut the whole cob into four equal pieces. Cut the pepper into 2·5-cm (1-in)

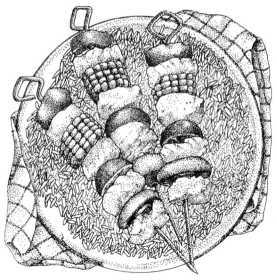

Marinated fish kebabs

squares. Thread the fish, sweetcorn, pepper, tomato halves and mushrooms on to four skewers. Cook under a hot grill for 15 minutes, turning the skewers occasionally and basting with the marinade.

Meanwhile, cook the rice in boiling salted water, with the turmeric added, for 10–12 minutes, until tender. Drain, spoon on to a warmed serving dish and arrange the kebabs on top. Pour over any remaining marinade from the grill pan.

○ *Calories 375 (1580)*

Plaice florentines

25 g (1 oz) Flora
700 g (1½ lb) plaice fillets, skinned and cut into bite-size pieces
grated rind and juice of ½ lemon
salt and freshly ground black pepper
15 g (½ oz) flour
300 ml (½ pint) skimmed milk
700 g (1½ lb) fresh spinach, washed and chopped
2 tomatoes, skinned and sliced
25 g (1 oz) fresh brown breadcrumbs
25 g (1 oz) Edam cheese, grated

Melt the margarine in a saucepan, add the fish with the lemon rind and juice and the

Pasta-topped Italian beef casserole *(page 72)*, Green beans and mushrooms in wine *(page 86)* ▶

seasoning and cook gently for 5 minutes. Remove the fish from the pan with a slotted spoon and reserve. Add the flour to the pan and cook for 1 minute. Gradually stir in the milk. Bring to the boil and cook for 1 minute, stirring. Carefully stir in the fish.

Cook the spinach in a little boiling salted water for 10 minutes until tender. Drain and chop finely. Arrange the spinach on the bottom of an ovenproof dish or four individual ovenproof cocottes. Cover with the tomato slices and pour over the fish and sauce. Sprinkle with the breadcrumbs, top with the cheese and cook in the oven at 190°C (375°F) mark 5 for about 15 minutes until the topping is golden brown.

Serve as a starter, or accompany with baked jacket potatoes for a light lunch.
○ *Calories 306 (1170)*

Plaice and cider bake

25 g (1 oz) Flora
1 medium onion, skinned and sliced
40 g (1½ oz) flour
300 ml (½ pint) dry cider
salt and freshly ground black pepper
350 g (12 oz) cooking apple, peeled, cored and sliced
900 g (2 lb) plaice fillets, skinned
25 g (1 oz) dry breadcrumbs
25 g (1 oz) Edam cheese, grated

Melt the margarine in a saucepan, add the onion and fry gently for 10 minutes. Stir in the flour and cook for 2 minutes. Add the cider, bring to the boil and cook for 3 minutes, stirring, until thickened. Season well. Place a layer of apple slices in the bottom of a shallow 1·7-litre (3-pint) ovenproof dish. Cover with half the fish fillets and pour over half the sauce. Repeat with the remaining apple, fish and sauce. Cover and cook in the oven at 180°C (350°F) mark 4 for 1 hour. Uncover, sprinkle with the breadcrumbs and cheese and place under a hot grill for about 5 minutes until golden brown.
○ *Calories 370 (1504)*

Haddock paprika

Illustrated in colour facing page 49

40 g (1½ oz) flour
15 ml (1 level tbsp) paprika
4 225-g (8-oz) haddock fillets, skinned
25 g (1 oz) Flora
10 ml (2 tsp) sunflower oil
1 small onion, skinned and chopped
1 red pepper, seeded and chopped
300 ml (½ pint) skimmed milk
150 ml (¼ pint) fish or chicken stock
salt and freshly ground black pepper
75 g (3 oz) button mushrooms, sliced

Mix together the flour and paprika and use to coat the fillets evenly. Heat the margarine and oil in a large frying pan. Fry the fish gently for 5 minutes on each side. Keep warm on a covered serving dish.

Add the onion and red pepper to the pan and fry for 5 minutes. Add any remaining flour to the pan and cook for 1 minute. Gradually stir in the milk and stock, bring to the boil, stirring, and cook for 3 minutes until thickened. Season, stir in the mushrooms and simmer gently for 5 minutes. Pour into a serving dish, arrange the fish on top and garnish with parsley if liked.
○ *Calories 311 (1249)*

Fisherman's pie

700 g (1½ lb) white fish
150 ml (¼ pint) skimmed milk
150 ml (¼ pint) dry white wine
1 bay leaf
6 black peppercorns
salt
25 g (1 oz) Flora
1 large onion, skinned and sliced
100 g (4 oz) button mushrooms, sliced
25 g (1 oz) flour
freshly ground white pepper
5 ml (1 level tsp) dried oregano
1·25 ml (¼ level tsp) caster sugar
225 g (8 oz) tomatoes, skinned and sliced
175 g (6 oz) all-in-one shortcrust pastry (see page 100)
1 egg white, lightly beaten

Glazed lemon tart *(page 94)*,
Quick strawberry cheesecake *(page 96)*

Place the fish in a shallow ovenproof dish, pour over the milk and wine and add the bay leaf, peppercorns and a pinch of salt. Cover and bake in the oven at 180°C (350°F) mark 4 for 20 minutes. Lift the fish from the cooking liquid with a fish slice or slotted spoon, remove the skin and bones and flake. Strain the cooking liquid and reserve.

Melt the margarine in a saucepan and fry the onion for 4 minutes. Add the mushrooms and cook for a further 2 minutes. Stir in the flour and cook for 1 minute, then gradually stir in the strained cooking liquid. Bring to the boil, stirring, and cook for 2 minutes until thickened. Add the seasoning, oregano and sugar.

Cover the bottom of a 1·2-litre (2-pint) pie dish with half the tomatoes. Season, place a layer of half the fish on top and pour over half the sauce. Repeat with the remaining tomatoes, fish and sauce. Roll out the pastry dough and use to cover the pie. Seal the edges well and flute. Brush with egg white and bake in the oven at 180°C (350°F) mark 4 for 35 minutes until golden brown.

◑ *Calories 571 (2294)*

Mushroom stuffed fish fillets

900 g (2 lb) plaice or sole fillets, skinned
300 ml (½ pint) filled milk (see page 116)
700 g (1½ lb) potatoes, cooked and mashed
1 egg white
15 g (½ oz) Flora
15 g (½ oz) flour
sprigs of parsley to garnish

For the stuffing
15 g (½ oz) Flora
1 small onion, skinned and finely chopped
175 g (6 oz) button mushrooms, finely
   chopped
25 g (1 oz) fresh white breadcrumbs
2·5 ml (½ level tsp) dried rosemary
salt and freshly ground black pepper

For the stuffing, melt the margarine in a saucepan, add the onion and fry for 10

minutes until soft. Add the mushrooms and cook for 2 minutes. Remove from the heat and stir in the breadcrumbs, rosemary and seasoning.

Divide the stuffing between the fillets and spread evenly. Roll up and secure with wooden cocktail sticks. Place the fillets in an ovenproof casserole and pour over the milk. Cover and bake in the oven at 180°C (350°F) mark 4 for 35 minutes.

While the fish is cooking, pipe the mashed potato round the edge of a flameproof dish, brush with the egg white and brown in the oven for 10–15 minutes. Remove the fish to the centre of the potato-edged dish, cover and keep warm. Reserve the cooking liquid.

Melt the remaining margarine in a pan, add the flour and cook for 3 minutes. Gradually stir in the strained cooking liquid, bring to the boil and cook for 3 minutes until thickened. Adjust the seasoning. Pour the sauce over the stuffed fillets and garnish with parsley sprigs.

○ *Calories 480 (1968)*

Salmon mousse with spring onion curls

15 g (½ oz) powdered gelatine
45 ml (3 tbsp) boiling water
2 213-g (7½-oz) cans red salmon
150 ml (¼ pint) skimmed milk
300 ml (½ pint) low fat natural yogurt
15 ml (1 tbsp) lemon juice
grated rind of ½ lemon
15 ml (1 level tbsp) tomato paste
salt and freshly ground white pepper
1·25 ml (¼ level tsp) ground mace
2 egg whites
bunch of spring onions

Dissolve the gelatine in the boiling water and cool. Mash the salmon with a fork or purée coarsely in a blender, with 30 ml (2 tbsp) of the liquid from the can and the milk. Pour into a mixing bowl and stir in the yogurt, juice and rind, tomato paste, seasoning and mace. Add the gelatine and stir thoroughly. Whisk the egg whites until stiff and fold into the salmon mixture. Pour into a 1·2-litre (2-pint) ring mould and leave to set.

Trim the spring onions and, holding the bulb end, make two or three lengthways cuts through the green leaves. Place in ice cold water and leave for about 30 minutes to curl. Turn out the mousse and fill the centre with the spring onion curls. *Serves 6*
○ *Calories 106 (438)*

Golden haddock soufflé

350 g (12 oz) smoked haddock or cod
300 ml (½ pint) skimmed milk
25 g (1 oz) Flora
25 g (1 oz) flour
freshly ground black pepper
100 g (4 oz) Edam cheese, grated
1 egg, separated
3 egg whites

In a large saucepan poach the fish in the milk for 5–8 minutes until tender. Remove the fish with a slotted spoon and flake

Golden haddock soufflé

coarsely. Strain the cooking liquid into a jug and reserve.

Melt the margarine in the saucepan, add the flour and cook for 1 minute. Stir in the cooking liquid, bring to the boil and simmer for 2 minutes. Remove from the heat, add the pepper and 75 g (3 oz) of the cheese. Stir in the fish and egg yolk. Whisk the four egg whites until stiff and fold into the fish mixture.

Spoon the mixture into a greased 900-ml (1½-pint) soufflé dish and cook in the oven at 190°C (375°F) mark 5 for 30–35 minutes until well risen and golden brown. Serve immediately, sprinkled with the remaining cheese.
◑ *Calories 282 (1107)*

Smoked mackerel and tomato salad

700 g (1½ lb) smoked mackerel
1 cos lettuce
450 g (1 lb) tomatoes, skinned, seeded and
    quartered
2 sticks of celery, washed and chopped
15 ml (1 tbsp) chopped fresh chives
15 ml (1 tbsp) chopped parsley
lemon wedges to garnish

For the dressing
45 ml (3 tbsp) vegetable oil
15 ml (1 tbsp) white wine vinegar
salt and freshly ground black pepper
1·25 ml (¼ level tsp) dry mustard

Remove the skin and bones from the fish, flake the flesh coarsely and place in a large bowl. Reserve four lettuce leaves for the base of the dish and shred the remaining leaves finely. Add to the bowl with the tomatoes, celery and chives.

Whisk the dressing ingredients together, add to the fish mixture and toss until evenly coated. Arrange the reserved lettuce leaves in a serving dish and spoon the fish mixture on top. Sprinkle with the parsley and garnish with lemon wedges.
○ *Calories 297 (1249)*

Dutch haddock flan

175 g (6 oz) all-in-one shortcrust pastry (see
  page 100)
15 g (½ oz) Flora
1 small onion, skinned and chopped
225 g (8 oz) smoked haddock, cooked and
  flaked
150 ml (¼ pint) low fat natural yogurt
150 ml (¼ pint) skimmed milk
100 g (4 oz) Edam cheese, grated
2·5 ml (½ level tsp) ground coriander
5 ml (1 level tsp) dry mustard
30 ml (2 tbsp) chopped fresh chives
salt and freshly ground white pepper
2 egg whites

Roll out the pastry dough and use to line a
21·5-cm (8½-in) flan ring. Bake blind in the
oven at 190°C (375°F) mark 5 for 10
minutes.

Melt the margarine in a frying pan, add
the onion and cook for 10 minutes until
soft. Mix together in a bowl the haddock,
yogurt, milk, half the cheese, the coriander,
mustard, chives, the fried onion and
seasoning. Whisk the egg whites until stiff
and fold into the fish mixture. Fill the flan
case with the haddock mixture and sprinkle
with the remaining cheese. Bake in the
oven for 25 minutes until the filling is set
and golden brown. *Serves 6*
◑ *Calories 337 (1325)*

Herrings with spinach

4 225-g (8-oz) herrings, cleaned
10 ml (2 tsp) sunflower oil
tomato wedges and watercress to garnish

For the stuffing
15 g (½ oz) Flora
1 medium onion, skinned and finely chopped
30 ml (2 level tbsp) tomato paste
50 g (2 oz) button mushrooms, finely
  chopped
2 tomatoes, skinned, seeded and chopped
225 g (8 oz) spinach, cooked and chopped
salt and freshly ground black pepper

For the stuffing, melt the margarine in a
saucepan, add the onion and fry gently for

10 minutes. Stir in the tomato paste, mushrooms, tomatoes, spinach and seasoning.

Stuff the herrings, brush lightly on both
sides with the oil and place in an ovenproof
dish. Cover with foil and cook in the oven at
180°C (350°F) mark 4 for 25 minutes.
Transfer to a heated serving dish and garnish with tomato wedges and watercress.
◑ *Calories 515 (2102)*

Stuffed cod cutlets with celery sauce

4 225-g (8-oz) cod cutlets
5 ml (1 tsp) sunflower oil

For the stuffing
50 g (2 oz) brown rice
15 g (½ oz) Flora
25 g (1 oz) onion, skinned and finely chopped
1 stick of celery, washed and finely chopped
1 red eating apple, cored and chopped
30 ml (2 tbsp) chopped parsley
30 ml (2 tbsp) chopped fresh chives
50 g (2 oz) walnuts, chopped
salt and freshly ground black pepper

For the sauce
1 cooking apple, peeled, cored and sliced
2 sticks of celery, washed and sliced
1 tomato, skinned, seeded and chopped
300 ml (½ pint) fish or chicken stock
15 ml (1 level tbsp) tomato paste
2·5 ml (½ level tsp) caster sugar

For the stuffing, cook the rice in boiling
salted water for 45 minutes, until just
tender. Drain well. Meanwhile, melt the
margarine in a frying pan, add the onion
and celery and fry gently for 15 minutes.
Stir in the rice, apple, herbs, walnuts and
seasoning and mix well.

Divide the stuffing into four and place on
top of the cod cutlets. Place the cutlets in a
roasting tin and brush the sides of the fish
with the oil. Cover with foil and cook in the
oven at 180°C (350°F) mark 4 for 25
minutes.

For the sauce, place all the ingredients in
a saucepan, cover and simmer gently for 45
minutes until all the vegetables are tender.

Purée the sauce in a blender or rub through a sieve. Serve the stuffed cutlets on a heated shallow dish, surrounded with the celery sauce.
○ *Calories 322 (1287)*

Halibut baked in a fish brick

15 ml (1 tbsp) vegetable oil
1 clove of garlic, skinned
900-g (2-lb) tail end of halibut or cod
15 ml (1 tbsp) wine vinegar
grated rind of 1 lemon
2·5 ml ($\frac{1}{2}$ level tsp) salt
freshly ground black pepper
5 ml (1 level tsp) dried rosemary

Brush the inside of the fish brick with the oil. Crush the garlic lightly and rub it over the inside of the brick. Cut the tail from the fish, remove the skin and place the fish in the bottom part of the brick. Sprinkle the remaining ingredients evenly over the fish. Put on the lid and bake in the oven at 150°C (300°F) mark 2 for 40–45 minutes. Serve with a fresh mixed salad and crusty bread.
○ *Calories 256 (1065)*

Muscadet casseroled plaice

15 g ($\frac{1}{2}$ oz) Flora
2 carrots, peeled and sliced
3 sticks of celery, washed and sliced
100 g (4 oz) button mushrooms, sliced
4 tomatoes, skinned, seeded and chopped
salt and freshly ground black pepper
900 g (2 lb) plaice fillets, skinned
150 ml ($\frac{1}{4}$ pint) Muscadet or dry white wine
150 ml ($\frac{1}{4}$ pint) fish or chicken stock
15 ml (1 level tbsp) cornflour
chopped parsley to garnish

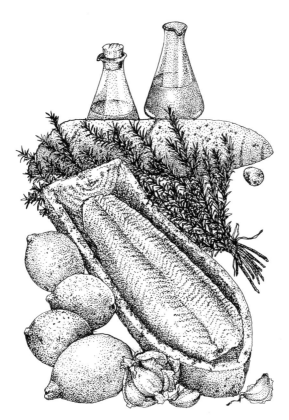

Halibut baked in a fish brick

Melt the margarine in frying pan, add the vegetables and seasoning and fry gently for 10 minutes. Place half of the vegetables in the bottom of a 1·4-litre (2½-pint) flame-proof casserole and cover with half the plaice fillets. Repeat with the remaining vegetables and fillets, and pour over the wine and stock. Cover and cook in the oven at 180°C (350°F) mark 4 for 30 minutes.

Lift out the plaice fillets and vegetables with a fish slice on to a heated serving dish. Cover and keep warm. Blend the cornflour to a smooth paste with a little water and stir into the remaining cooking liquid. Bring to the boil, stirring, and cook for 3 minutes until thickened. Pour the sauce over the fish and sprinkle with parsley to serve.
○ *Calories 260 (1086)*

Savoury fish tricorns

225 g (8 oz) all-in-one shortcrust pastry (see page 100)
450 g (1 lb) cod or haddock fillet, skinned
25 g (1 oz) Flora
25 g (1 oz) flour
300 ml (½ pint) skimmed milk
grated rind of 1 lemon
15 ml (1 tbsp) lemon juice
45 ml (3 tbsp) chopped parsley
5 ml (1 level tsp) salt
freshly ground black pepper
skimmed milk to glaze

Roll out the pastry dough and cut out four large rounds with a 16-cm (6½-in) saucer.

Cut the fish into 2·5-cm (1-in) cubes. Melt the margarine in a large saucepan, add the fish and cook gently for 2–3 minutes. Remove from the pan and reserve. Stir the flour into the pan juices and cook for 2 minutes. Gradually stir in the milk. Bring to the boil, stirring, and cook for 2 minutes. Add the lemon rind and juice, parsley and seasoning and return the fish to the pan.

Spoon the fish filling into the centre of the pastry circles. Dampen the edges with a little water, then gather up the pastry over the filling and pinch the edges together to form tricorn shapes. Place on a greased baking sheet and brush with a little milk to glaze. Bake in the oven at 190°C (375°F) mark 5 for 25–30 minutes until golden brown.
◑ *Calories 599 (2336)*

Spicy fish stuffed tomatoes

8 large tomatoes, skinned
450 g (1 lb) whiting or haddock fillet, skinned
25 g (1 oz) Flora
1 small onion, skinned and chopped
1 clove of garlic, skinned and crushed
pinch chilli powder
2·5 ml (½ level tsp) ground coriander
5 ml (1 level tsp) salt
freshly ground black pepper
25 g (1 oz) long grain rice, cooked
300 ml (½ pint) fish or chicken stock
25 g (1 oz) flour
30 ml (2 level tbsp) tomato paste
10 ml (2 tsp) Worcestershire sauce

Cut the top off each tomato and scoop out the seeds. Cut the fish into 2·5-cm (1-in) cubes.

Melt the margarine in a large saucepan and fry the onion and garlic for 5 minutes. Add the spices and seasoning and cook for a further 2 minutes. Stir in the rice and fish and cook for 5 minutes. Spoon into the tomato cups and place in an ovenproof dish. Pour the stock around the tomatoes and cover with foil. Cook in the oven at 180°C (350°F) mark 4 for 25–30 minutes until the tomatoes are tender. Remove the tomatoes to a heated serving dish and keep warm.

In a bowl, blend the flour to a smooth paste with a little water. Add the tomato paste and Worcestershire sauce and gradually blend in the cooking liquid. Pour into a saucepan, bring to the boil, stirring, and cook for 3–4 minutes until thickened. Pour the sauce over the stuffed tomatoes before serving
○ *Calories 205 (798)*

Cod cutlets with Jerusalem artichoke sauce

450 g (1 lb) Jerusalem artichokes, peeled and
   sliced
salt
1 slice of lemon
4 225-g (8-oz) cod cutlets
1 bay leaf
6 peppercorns
4 cloves
freshly ground white pepper
3 tomatoes, skinned, seeded and chopped
30 ml (2 level tbsp) tomato paste
300 ml ($\frac{1}{2}$ pint) skimmed milk
tomato slices and watercress to garnish

Put the artichokes immediately into a large pan containing salted water and a slice of lemon. Bring to the boil and cook for 10–12 minutes; drain well.

Place the fish in an ovenproof dish, add the artichokes, bay leaf, peppercorns, cloves, seasoning and tomatoes. Stir the tomato paste into the milk and pour over the fish. Cover and cook in the oven at 180°C (350°F) mark 4 for 25 minutes.

Transfer the cutlets to a heated serving dish, cover and keep warm. Remove the bay leaf, peppercorns and cloves from the milk. Purée the milk and vegetables in a blender or rub through a sieve. Pour the sauce around the fish and garnish with tomato slices and watercress.
○ *Calories 209 (861)*

Soused cod with apple

2 medium cooking apples, peeled, cored and
   sliced
4 175-g (6-oz) cod steaks
1 large onion, skinned and thinly sliced
2 bay leaves
5 ml (1 level tsp) pickling spice
20 ml (4 level tsp) demerara sugar
150 ml ($\frac{1}{4}$ pint) water
150 ml ($\frac{1}{4}$ pint) cider vinegar
2·5 ml ($\frac{1}{2}$ level tsp) mixed spice
2·5 ml ($\frac{1}{2}$ level tsp) salt
freshly ground black pepper
chopped parsley and lemon slices to garnish

Place half the apple rings in the bottom of a large ovenproof dish. Place the cod steaks on top and cover with the remaining apple and the onion slices. Tie the bay leaves and pickling spice in a muslin bag and add to the dish. Add the sugar, water, cider vinegar, mixed spice and seasoning. Cover with foil and cook in the oven at 150°C (300°F) mark 2 for 40–45 minutes.

Remove the fish to a heated serving dish with a slotted spoon and keep warm. Remove the bag of spices. Purée half the apple and onion slices with all the liquid in a blender or rub through a sieve. Reheat with the remaining apple and onion slices and pour this sauce over the fish on the serving dish. Garnish with chopped parsley and lemon slices.
○ *Calories 161 (681)*

Meat and Poultry

Pasta-topped Italian beef casserole

Illustrated in colour facing page 64

900 g (2 lb) chuck steak
15 ml (1 tbsp) sunflower oil
1 medium onion, skinned and sliced
1 clove of garlic, skinned and crushed
225 g (8 oz) tomatoes, skinned, seeded and
    chopped
30 ml (2 level tbsp) tomato paste
4 sticks of celery, washed and sliced
150 ml ($\frac{1}{4}$ pint) dry red wine
300 ml ($\frac{1}{2}$ pint) beef stock
salt and freshly ground black pepper
5 ml (1 level tsp) dried oregano
1 bay leaf
10 ml (2 level tsp) cornflour
225 g (8 oz) pasta spirals
25 g (1 oz) Edam cheese, grated

Remove all visible fat from the beef, then cut the beef into 5-cm (2-in) cubes. Heat the oil in a large pan, add the beef, onion and garlic and fry gently for 10 minutes. Add the tomatoes, tomato paste, celery, wine, stock, seasoning, oregano and bay leaf. Blend the cornflour to a smooth paste with a little water and stir into the pan. Bring to the boil, stirring until thickened. Pour into an ovenproof casserole, cover and cook in the oven at 170°C (325°F) mark 3 for 2 hours.

Cook the pasta in boiling salted water for 15 minutes; drain well. Remove the bay leaf from the casserole and spoon the pasta over the top. Sprinkle with the grated cheese, return to the oven and continue cooking, uncovered, for about another 30 minutes until the pasta topping is golden brown.

⬤ *Calories 572 (2378)*

Beef and mushroom loaf

15 g ($\frac{1}{2}$ oz) Flora
1 large onion, skinned and finely chopped
1 clove of garlic, skinned and crushed
100 g (4 oz) button mushrooms, sliced
700 g (1$\frac{1}{2}$ lb) braising steak
100 g (4 oz) fresh white breadcrumbs
225 g (8 oz) tomatoes, skinned and chopped
45 ml (3 level tbsp) tomato paste
60 ml (4 tbsp) dry red wine
1 egg white
5 ml (1 level tsp) salt
freshly ground black pepper
5 ml (1 tsp) sunflower oil

72

Melt the margarine in a frying pan, add the onion and garlic and fry for 10 minutes. Remove from the pan and place in a large mixing bowl. Add the mushrooms to the pan and fry gently for 5 minutes. Drain and reserve. Cut all visible fat from the beef then mince it and add to the onion in the bowl. Stir in the remaining ingredients except the oil and mix well.

Grease the bottom and sides of a 900-g (2-lb) loaf tin with the oil. Line the bottom of the tin with greased greaseproof paper. Spoon in half the mince mixture and press down firmly. Add the mushrooms in a layer, then the remaining mince, smoothing the top. Cook in the oven at 180°C (350°F) mark 4 for 1 hour. Turn out and serve with Herby tomato sauce (see page 113).

◐ *Calories 444 (1847)*

Beef moussaka

450 g (1 lb) aubergines
3 medium courgettes, trimmed
700 g (1½ lb) braising steak
1 large onion, skinned and chopped
1 clove of garlic, skinned and crushed
salt and freshly ground black pepper
30 ml (2 level tbsp) tomato paste
4 large tomatoes, skinned and sliced
30 ml (2 tbsp) beef stock
300 ml (½ pint) all-in-one coating cheese
   sauce (see page 114)
25 g (1 oz) Edam cheese, grated

Cut the aubergines and courgettes into 0·5-cm (¼-in) slices, place in a colander or sieve and sprinkle with salt. Leave for 30 minutes, then rinse and dry thoroughly.

Meanwhile, cut any visible fat from the steak and mince it. Fry the minced beef, onion, garlic and seasoning in a non-stick frying pan for 5 minutes until the meat has browned. Stir in the tomato paste. Place a layer of tomatoes over the bottom of a large ovenproof casserole, spoon over half the mince mixture and cover with a layer of courgettes and aubergines, seasoning each layer well. Repeat the layering with the remaining ingredients then spoon over the stock and the cheese sauce. Cover and cook in the oven at 180°C (350°F) mark 4 for 50 minutes. Remove the lid, sprinkle over the cheese and return to the oven to cook for about 15 minutes until golden brown.

● *Calories 487 (2027)*

Mustardy braised sirloin

900-g (2-lb) piece beef sirloin, boned
15 g (½ oz) Flora
225 g (8 oz) carrots, peeled and diced
225 g (8 oz) leeks, sliced and washed
3 sticks of celery, washed and sliced
300 ml (½ pint) beef stock
10 ml (2 level tsp) cornflour
watercress to garnish

For the mustard filling
15 g (½ oz) Flora
1 medium onion, skinned and finely chopped
50 g (2 oz) mushrooms, chopped
5 ml (1 level tsp) caraway seeds
45 ml (3 level tbsp) Dijon mustard
salt and freshly ground black pepper

For the filling, melt the margarine in a frying pan and fry the onion gently for 15 minutes. Add the mushrooms, caraway seeds, mustard and seasoning and fry for 3 minutes.

Lay the beef out flat and spread with the mustard filling. Roll up from one of the short edges and secure with string. Melt the margarine in a flameproof casserole and add the carrots, leeks and celery. Fry gently for 15 minutes and season well. Place the beef on top and pour over the stock. Cover and cook in the oven at 180°C (350°F) mark 4 for 1 hour.

Remove the beef to a heated serving dish, cover and keep warm. Blend the cornflour to a smooth paste with a little water and stir into the vegetables and stock. Bring to the boil, stirring, and cook for 3 minutes until thickened. Remove the string and slice the beef. Spoon the vegetable mixture around the beef and garnish with watercress.

● *Calories 637 (2595)*

Crispy cottage pie

700 g (1½ lb) braising steak
1 large onion, skinned and chopped
100 g (4 oz) carrot, peeled and finely diced
100 g (4 oz) turnip, peeled and finely diced
salt and freshly ground black pepper
10 ml (2 tsp) Worcestershire sauce
15 ml (1 level tbsp) sweet pickle
15 g (½ oz) flour
300 ml (½ pint) beef stock
4 25-g (1-oz) slices of white bread
25 g (1 oz) Flora

Remove any visible fat from the beef and
mince it. Fry the minced beef in a large non-
stick frying pan for 10 minutes until brown.
Add the onion, carrot, turnip and seasoning and cook, covered, for 10 minutes. Stir
in the Worcestershire sauce, pickle and
flour and cook for another 2 minutes. Stir in
the stock and bring to the boil, stirring.
Spoon into a 1·4-litre (2½-pint) ovenproof
dish.

Cut the slices of bread in half diagonally
and spread with the margarine. Arrange
the bread on the top of the mince, margarine side up. Bake in the oven at 180°C
(350°F) mark 4 for 50 minutes until the
bread is crisp and golden brown.
◑ *Calories 469 (1922)*

Stuffed aubergines

75 g (3 oz) brown rice
2 450-g (1-lb) aubergines
salt
700 g (1½ lb) lean chuck steak
1 medium onion, skinned and chopped
4 tomatoes, skinned, seeded and chopped
30 ml (2 level tbsp) tomato paste
10 ml (2 tsp) Worcestershire sauce
freshly ground black pepper
150 ml (¼ pint) beef stock
15 g (½ oz) fresh white breadcrumbs
25 g (1 oz) Edam cheese, grated

Cook the rice in boiling salted water for 45
minutes and drain. Meanwhile, cut the
aubergines in half and scoop out the flesh,
leaving a 0·5-cm (¼-in) shell. Sprinkle the

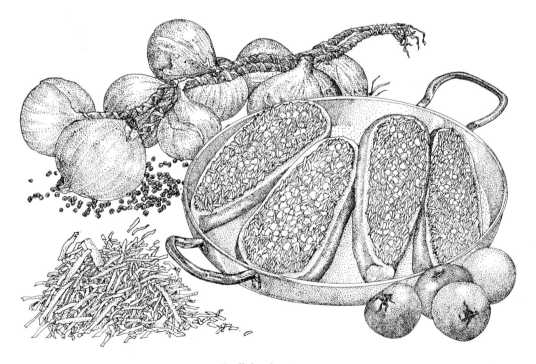

Stuffed aubergines

shells and flesh with salt. Leave for 30 minutes, then rinse thoroughly and dry with kitchen paper towel. Chop the flesh.

Cut any visible fat from the beef and mince it. Fry the beef and onion in a large non-stick frying pan for 15 minutes. Add the tomatoes, tomato paste, Worcestershire sauce, seasoning, chopped aubergine flesh and stock. Mix well and cook for 2 minutes.

Spoon the beef filling into the aubergine shells, place in a roasting tin and cook in the oven at 180°C (350°F) mark 4 for 35 minutes. Stir together the breadcrumbs and cheese and sprinkle over the aubergines. Return to the oven and cook for a further 10 minutes. Lift on to a heated dish. Serve with Herby tomato sauce (see page 113).

◗ *Calories 410 (1726)*

Beef in vermouth marinade

900 g (2 lb) top rib of beef
15 g ($\frac{1}{2}$ oz) Flora
300 ml ($\frac{1}{2}$ pint) beef stock
15 ml (1 level tbsp) cornflour
sprigs of parsley to garnish

For the marinade
1 bay leaf
2·5 ml ($\frac{1}{2}$ level tsp) dried rosemary
1 large onion, skinned and chopped
100 g (4 oz) carrot, peeled and sliced
1 large leek, sliced and washed
45 ml (3 tbsp) sunflower oil
30 ml (2 tbsp) wine vinegar
30 ml (2 tbsp) dry vermouth
salt and freshly ground black pepper

Trim all visible fat from the beef and cut into 2·5-cm (1-in) cubes. Place in a large bowl with the marinade ingredients. Cover and leave in the refrigerator overnight.

Drain the beef and reserve the marinade. Melt the margarine in a flameproof casserole, add the beef and cook for 10 minutes until browned all over. Add the reserved marinade and stock and bring to the boil. Cover and cook in the oven at 170°C (325°F) mark 3 for 2 hours.

Blend the cornflour to a smooth paste

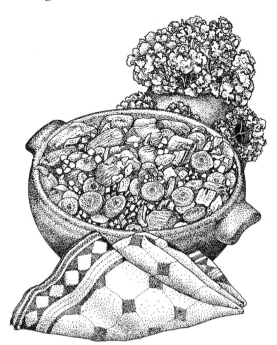

Beef in vermouth marinade

with a little water and stir into the casserole. Bring to the boil, stirring, and cook for 3 minutes until thickened. Garnish with sprigs of parsley.

● *Calories 652 (2662)*

Beef and anchovy roulades

4 175-g (6-oz) slices beef topside, beaten
15 g ($\frac{1}{2}$ oz) Flora
300 ml ($\frac{1}{2}$ pint) beef stock
4 tomatoes, skinned, seeded and chopped
30 ml (2 level tbsp) tomato paste
salt and freshly ground black pepper
15 ml (1 level tbsp) cornflour
watercress to garnish

For the filling
8 anchovy fillets
45 ml (3 tbsp) skimmed milk
15 g ($\frac{1}{2}$ oz) Flora
1 medium onion, skinned and finely chopped
10 ml (2 level tsp) capers, chopped
2·5 ml ($\frac{1}{2}$ tsp) anchovy essence
salt and freshly ground black pepper

For the filling, soak the anchovy fillets in the milk for about 1 hour. Melt the margarine in a large frying pan, add the onion and fry gently for 15 minutes. Drain and chop the anchovy fillets and stir into the onion with the capers, anchovy essence and seasoning.

Spread the filling over the beaten-out slices of beef. Roll up and secure with string or wooden cocktail sticks. Melt the margarine in the frying pan, add the beef roulades and fry for 10 minutes until brown on all sides. Add the stock, chopped tomatoes, tomato paste and seasoning to the pan. Cover and simmer gently for 50 minutes. Remove the beef roulades to a heated serving dish, cover and keep warm.

Blend the cornflour to a smooth paste with a little water and stir into the cooking liquid. Bring to the boil, stirring, and cook for 3 minutes until thickened. Remove the string or cocktail sticks from the beef and pour over the sauce. Garnish with sprigs of watercress.

◉ *Calories 523 (1968)*

Veal tagliatelle

15 g (½ oz) Flora
1 large onion, skinned and chopped
2 cloves of garlic, skinned and crushed
396-g (14-oz) can tomatoes
about 150 ml (¼ pint) red wine
30 ml (2 level tbsp) tomato paste
2·5 ml (½ level tsp) caster sugar
bay leaf
5 ml (1 level tsp) salt
freshly ground black pepper
225 g (8 oz) button mushrooms, sliced
700 g (1½ lb) cooked lean veal, diced
100 g (4 oz) frozen peas
225 g (8 oz) tagliatelle
15 g (½ oz) grated Parmesan cheese

Melt the margarine in a large saucepan, add the onion and garlic and fry gently for 10 minutes until soft. Strain the tomatoes and reserve the juice, making it up to 300 ml (½ pint) with red wine. Roughly chop the tomatoes and add to the onion with the juice and wine. Add the tomato paste, sugar, bay leaf and seasoning. Cover and simmer gently for 20 minutes. Stir in the mushrooms, veal and peas and continue cooking for 15 minutes.

Meanwhile cook the tagliatelle in boiling salted water for 15 minutes. Drain and spoon around the edge of a heated shallow serving dish. Remove the bay leaf from the sauce and pour into the centre of the pasta ring. Sprinkle with the Parmesan cheese before serving.

◑ *Calories 391 (1651)*

Veal and mustard olives

50 g (2 oz) Flora
30 ml (2 level tbsp) Dijon mustard
2·5 ml (½ level tsp) paprika
salt and freshly ground black pepper
4 175-g (6-oz) veal escalopes, beaten
1 large onion, skinned and sliced
225 g (8 oz) tomatoes, skinned and sliced
30 ml (2 level tbsp) tomato paste
5 ml (1 level tsp) caster sugar
1 bay leaf
25 g (1 oz) flour
150 ml (¼ pint) chicken stock
150 ml (¼ pint) dry red wine
watercress to garnish

In a small bowl mix together 40 g (1½ oz) of the margarine and the mustard, paprika and seasoning. Lay the beaten-out escalopes flat and spread with the savoury margarine. Roll up each escalope and secure with wooden cocktail sticks.

Melt the remaining margarine in a large frying pan. Add the veal rolls and fry gently for 4 minutes until browned on all sides. Remove from the pan and place in an ovenproof casserole. Add the onion and tomatoes to the frying pan, cover and fry gently for 10 minutes. Stir in the tomato paste, sugar and bay leaf. Sprinkle over the flour and cook, stirring, for 2 minutes. Gradually stir in the stock and wine and bring to the boil, stirring. Adjust the

Veal and mustard olives

and cook in the oven at 180°C (350°F) mark 4 for 1¾–2 hours. Remove the lemon wedges and serve garnished with fresh lemon twists and watercress.
◗ *Calories 336 (1371)*

Veal and mushroom pie

700 g (1½ lb) lean pie veal
30 ml (2 level tbsp) seasoned flour
25 g (1 oz) Flora
1 large onion, skinned and chopped
1 clove of garlic, skinned and crushed
150 ml (¼ pint) chicken stock
225 g (8 oz) button mushrooms, sliced
30 ml (2 level tbsp) capers, chopped
salt and freshly ground black pepper
175 g (6 oz) all-in-one shortcrust pastry (see page 100)
1 egg white, beaten

Trim any visible fat from the meat and cut into 2·5-cm (1-in) cubes. Toss the veal in seasoned flour. Melt the margarine in a large frying pan, add the veal, onion and garlic and fry gently for 10 minutes. Stir in the stock, bring to the boil and stir until thickened. Add the mushrooms, capers and seasoning. Pour into a 1·4-litre (2½-pint) pie dish.

Roll out the pastry dough and use to cover the pie dish. Seal and flute the edges. Brush the top with egg white and bake in the oven at 180°C (350°F) mark 4 for 45 minutes.
◉ *Calories 619 (2499)*

Veal escalopes in wine

15 g (½ oz) Flora
1 small onion, skinned and sliced
100 g (4 oz) button mushrooms, wiped
4 225-g (8-oz) veal escalopes, trimmed
150 ml (¼ pint) dry white wine
150 ml (¼ pint) chicken stock
350 g (12 oz) cooking apples, peeled, cored and thinly sliced
salt and freshly ground white pepper
10 ml (2 level tsp) cornflour
chopped parsley to garnish

seasoning and pour the sauce over the veal. Cover and cook in the oven at 170°C (325°F) mark 3 for 1 hour. Before serving, remove the bay leaf and cocktail sticks and garnish with watercress.
◗ *Calories 406 (1642)*

Veal in raisin sauce

700 g (1½ lb) lean pie veal
25 g (1 oz) Flora
1 medium onion, skinned and chopped
25 g (1 oz) flour
400 ml (¾ pint) chicken stock
225 g (8 oz) button mushrooms
75 g (3 oz) raisins
5 ml (1 level tsp) salt
freshly ground black pepper
2 lemon wedges
lemon twists and watercress to garnish

Trim any visible fat from the meat and cut into 2·5-cm (1-in) cubes. Melt the margarine in a flameproof casserole and fry the onion for 5 minutes. Add the meat to the pan and fry for a further 5 minutes. Remove the onion and meat and reserve.

Stir the flour into the remaining juices and cook for 1 minute. Gradually stir in the stock, bring to the boil and cook for 2 minutes. Add the mushrooms, raisins and seasoning and return the onion and meat to the casserole. Bring to the boil, push the lemon wedges well into the casserole, cover

Melt the margarine in a frying pan, add the vegetables and cover and fry gently for 20 minutes. Remove from the pan with a draining spoon and reserve. Add the veal and fry for 2 minutes on each side. Return the vegetables to the pan with the wine, stock, apples, and seasoning. Cover and simmer gently for 10 minutes.

Place the veal on a heated serving dish, cover and keep warm. Blend the cornflour to a smooth paste with a little water and stir into the cooking liquid. Bring to the boil, stirring, and cook for 2 minutes until thickened. Pour over the veal and sprinkle with parsley.

◗ *Calories 331 (1350)*

Spiced veal with aubergines

450 g (1 lb) aubergines, sliced
salt
900 g (2 lb) lean pie veal
25 g (1 oz) Flora
1 large onion, skinned and chopped
5 ml (1 level tsp) ground turmeric
5 ml (1 level tsp) chilli seasoning
5 ml (1 level tsp) ground cumin
5 ml (1 level tsp) salt
15 ml (1 level tbsp) curry paste
30 ml (2 level tbsp) mango chutney
50 g (2 oz) sultanas
15 ml (1 tbsp) Worcestershire sauce
300 ml ($\frac{1}{2}$ pint) chicken stock
15 ml (1 level tbsp) cornflour
watercress to garnish

Sprinkle the aubergines with salt and leave for 30 minutes. Rinse thoroughly and dry with kitchen paper towel.

Trim any visible fat from the veal and cut into 2·5-cm (1-in) cubes. Melt the margarine in a large saucepan and fry the aubergines for 5 minutes until soft. Remove from the pan with a slotted spoon and reserve. Fry the onion for 5 minutes. Add the veal and continue frying for 10 minutes until browned. Stir in the spices, salt and curry paste and cook for 5 minutes, stirring. Add the chutney, sultanas, Worcester-

shire sauce and stock, then return the aubergines and simmer gently for 1$\frac{1}{4}$ hours.

Blend the cornflour to a smooth paste with a little water and stir into the veal. Bring to the boil, stirring, and cook for 3 minutes until thickened. Spoon into a heated serving dish and garnish with watercress.

◗ *Calories 461 (1868)*

Lamb chops braised in beer

15 g ($\frac{1}{2}$ oz) Flora
1 large onion, skinned and chopped
1 clove of garlic, skinned and crushed
225 g (8 oz) swede, peeled and diced
225 g (8 oz) carrots, peeled and diced
100 g (4 oz) parsnip, peeled and diced
4 225-g (8-oz) lamb chump chops
150 ml ($\frac{1}{4}$ pint) brown ale
150 ml ($\frac{1}{4}$ pint) beef stock
5 ml (1 level tsp) dried rosemary
5 ml (1 level tsp) sugar
salt and freshly ground black pepper
2 tomatoes, skinned, seeded and chopped
10 ml (2 level tsp) cornflour
watercress to garnish

Melt the margarine in a large frying pan and fry the vegetables for 10 minutes. Place in the bottom of a flameproof casserole. Trim any visible fat from the chops and add to the frying pan. Cook for 5 minutes on each side and place on top of the vegetables. Pour over the ale and stock, add the rosemary and sugar and season well. Cover and bake in the oven at 180°C (350°F) mark 4 for about 1$\frac{1}{2}$ hours. Remove the lid, add the tomatoes and continue cooking for 15 minutes.

Remove the chops and spoon the vegetables into a heated shallow serving dish. Place the chops on top. Blend the cornflour to a smooth paste with a little water and add to the cooking liquid in the casserole. Bring to the boil and stir until thickened. Pour over the lamb and vegetables. Garnish with sprigs of watercress.

◗ *Calories 521 (2135)*

Sherried chump chops with mushrooms

15 g (½ oz) Flora
1 large onion, skinned and sliced
4 225-g (8-oz) lamb chump chops
225 g (8 oz) button mushrooms, sliced
300 ml (½ pint) beef stock
60 ml (4 tbsp) dry sherry
10 ml (2 tsp) soy sauce
5 ml (1 level tsp) caster sugar
2·5 ml (½ level tsp) ground cinnamon
salt and freshly ground black pepper
15 ml (1 level tbsp) cornflour
watercress to garnish

Melt the margarine in a large frying pan, add the onion and cook for 5 minutes. Trim any visible fat from the chops and add to the pan. Cook for 3 minutes on each side. Add the mushrooms, stock, sherry, soy sauce, sugar, cinnamon and seasoning. Stir well, cover and simmer gently for 45 minutes.

Remove the chops to a heated serving dish, cover and keep warm. Bring the cooking liquid to the boil and boil rapidly for 10 minutes to reduce by half. Blend the cornflour to a smooth paste with a little water and stir into the reduced liquid. Simmer for 2 minutes, stirring until thickened. Pour over the lamb chops and garnish with watercress.

◑ *Calories 496 (2044)*

Lamb chops in lemon ginger sauce

25 g (1 oz) Flora
1 medium onion, skinned and chopped
4 lamb chump chops
15 ml (1 level tbsp) flour
400 ml (¾ pint) beef stock
5 ml (1 level tsp) salt
freshly ground black pepper
60 ml (4 tbsp) lemon juice
grated rind of 1 lemon
30 ml (2 level tbsp) ginger marmalade
5 ml (1 level tsp) ground ginger
lemon slices and watercress to garnish

Melt the margarine in a frying pan and fry the onion for 5 minutes. Trim any visible fat from the chops, add to the pan and fry on each side for 5 minutes. Remove the chops and reserve.

Stir the flour into the pan juices and cook for 1 minute. Gradually add the stock, bring to the boil, stirring, and cook for 2 minutes. Add the remaining ingredients and replace the chops. Cover and simmer gently for 30 minutes until the chops are tender. Serve garnished with lemon twists and watercress.

◑ *Calories 538 (2177)*

Marinated lamb with orange mint sauce

4 225-g (8-oz) lamb chump chops
juice from 2 oranges
30 ml (2 tbsp) chopped fresh mint
15 ml (1 tbsp) sunflower oil
1 large onion, skinned and chopped
300 ml (½ pint) beef stock
salt and freshly ground white pepper
15 ml (1 level tbsp) cornflour
orange slices and sprigs of fresh mint to
    garnish

Trim any visible fat from the chops and make two slashes 1 cm (½ in) deep on each side. Place in a shallow dish, pour over the orange juice and sprinkle with the mint. Cover and leave to marinate for 1 hour, turning the chops after 30 minutes.

Heat the oil in a flameproof casserole, add the chops and onion and fry gently for 10 minutes until brown. Pour over the marinade, stock and seasoning. Cover and cook in the oven at 180°C (350°F) mark 4 for 1½ hours.

Remove the chops to a heated serving dish and keep hot. Blend the cornflour to a smooth paste with a little water and stir into the cooking liquid in the casserole. Bring to the boil, stirring, and cook for 3 minutes until thickened. Pour this sauce over the chops. Garnish with orange slices and sprigs of mint.

◑ *Calories 473 (1960)*

Lamb casseroled in red wine

Lamb casseroled in red wine

700-g (1½-lb) boned leg of lamb
30 ml (2 level tbsp) seasoned flour
25 g (1 oz) Flora
2 medium onions, skinned and chopped
3 sticks of celery, washed and thinly sliced.
225 g (8 oz) carrots, peeled and sliced
150 ml (¼ pint) red wine
400 ml (¾ pint) beef stock
396-g (14-oz) can tomatoes
10 ml (2 level tsp) dried marjoram
2·5 ml (½ level tsp) sugar
salt and freshly ground pepper

Trim all visible fat from the lamb, cut into 2·5-cm (1-in) cubes and toss in seasoned flour. Heat half the margarine in a frying pan and cook the onions, celery and carrots for 10 minutes until soft. Place in an ovenproof casserole.

Melt the remaining margarine in the pan, cook the lamb for 10 minutes until browned and add to the casserole. Add the wine and stock to the pan and stir to loosen any residue. Add the tomatoes with their juice, the marjoram, sugar and seasoning and bring to the boil. Pour into the casserole and stir until well blended. Cook in the oven at 180°C (350°F) mark 4 for 2 hours.
◗ *Calories 585 (2482)*

Lamb with lentils and carrots

700 g (1½ lb) lean boned lamb
15 ml (1 tbsp) vegetable oil
100 g (4 oz) lentils, soaked overnight
450 g (1 lb) carrots, peeled and sliced
2 onions, skinned and sliced
5 ml (1 level tsp) salt
freshly ground black pepper
5 ml (1 level tsp) grated nutmeg
1 bay leaf
15 ml (1 level tbsp) tomato paste
400 ml (¾ pint) beef stock
chopped parsley to garnish

Trim any visible fat from the lamb and cut into 2·5-cm (1-in) cubes. Heat the oil in a frying pan and fry the lamb for 10 minutes until browned. Place in an ovenproof casserole with the drained lentils.

Add the carrots and onions to the frying pan and fry for 10 minutes. Add the remaining ingredients to the pan and bring to the boil, stirring. Pour into the casserole and stir until well blended. Cover and cook in the oven at 180°C (350°F) mark 4 for 1½ hours. Remove the bay leaf and sprinkle with parsley.
◗ *Calories 543 (2311)*

Chicken and leek rissoles

350 g (12 oz) potatoes, peeled and quartered
15 g (½ oz) Flora
1 medium onion, skinned and finely chopped
100 g (4 oz) leek, finely chopped and washed
30 ml (2 tbsp) chopped parsley
2·5 ml (½ level tsp) salt
freshly ground black pepper
700 g (1½ lb) raw chicken meat, minced
30 ml (2 tbsp) sunflower oil

Date crunchies *(page 102)*, Peanut butter cookies *(page 105)*,
Applenut spice squares *(page 103)*

Cook the potatoes in boiling salted water for 20 minutes until tender. Drain well and mash. Meanwhile, melt the margarine in a frying pan, add the onion and leek and fry gently for 10 minutes. Stir the onion mixture into the mashed potato with the parsley, seasoning and chicken. Mix well, divide into eight and shape into rounds. Chill for 20 minutes.

Heat the oil in a frying pan and fry the rissoles for 12 minutes on each side until golden brown. Drain on kitchen paper towel. Serve with Herby tomato sauce or Spiced aubergine (see pages 113 and 86).
○ *Calories 309 (1417)*

Spicy boned chicken

1·6-kg (3½-lb) chicken, boned
5 ml (1 tsp) sunflower oil
watercress to garnish

For the stuffing
15 g (½ oz) Flora
1 small onion, skinned and chopped
100 g (4 oz) mushrooms, chopped
1·25 ml (¼ level tsp) ground coriander
1·25 ml (¼ level tsp) turmeric
1·25 ml (¼ level tsp) ground cardamom
1·25 ml (¼ level tsp) salt
freshly ground black pepper
100 g (4 oz) fresh white breadcrumbs
grated rind of 1 lemon
30 ml (2 tbsp) lemon juice
30 ml (2 level tbsp) low fat natural yogurt

For the stuffing, melt the margarine in a frying pan, add the onion and fry for 4 minutes until soft. Add the mushrooms, coriander, turmeric, cardamom, salt and pepper and cook for 2 minutes. In a bowl, mix together the breadcrumbs, lemon rind, lemon juice and yogurt and add the mushroom mixture.

Lay the chicken out flat and spoon the stuffing down the centre. Fold the sides of the chicken over the stuffing and sew up, using string and a trussing needle.

Place the chicken in a roasting tin, join side down, and brush with the oil. Cook in

the oven at 180°C (350°F) mark 4 for about 1½ hours until golden brown. This can be served hot but is best if refrigerated overnight, then sliced and garnished with watercress. *Serves 6*
◗ *Calories 345 (1404)*

Crunchy chicken salad

225 g (8 oz) red cabbage, shredded
225 g (8 oz) bean sprouts
700 g (1½ lb) cooked chicken meat, diced
50 g (2 oz) peanuts
2 red eating apples, cored and diced
30 ml (2 tbsp) lemon juice

For the dressing
90 ml (6 tbsp) dry sherry
30 ml (2 tbsp) soy sauce
30 ml (2 tbsp) wine vinegar
5 ml (1 level tsp) caster sugar

In a small bowl whisk together the dressing ingredients. Cook the cabbage in boiling salted water for 2 minutes, drain well and place in a large bowl. While still warm, pour over the dressing, cover and chill for 30 minutes.

Stir the bean sprouts, chicken and peanuts into the cabbage mixture. Toss the apples in the lemon juice and add to the salad. Chill for 15 minutes and spoon into a serving dish.
○ *Calories 357 (1379)*

Mustardy chicken casserole

25 g (1 oz) Flora
1 large onion, skinned and sliced
2 leeks, sliced and washed
100 g (4 oz) button mushrooms, sliced
salt and freshly ground black pepper
30 ml (2 level tbsp) Dijon mustard
4 225-g (8-oz) chicken breast portions,
    skinned and boned
150 ml (¼ pint) chicken stock
150 ml (¼ pint) dry white wine
60 ml (4 level tbsp) low fat natural yogurt
watercress to garnish

Melt the margarine in a heavy flameproof

Paella *(page 108)*, Garlic bread *(page 111)*

casserole. Fry the onion and leeks for 4 minutes. Add the mushrooms and fry for 2 minutes. Season well. Spread the mustard over the chicken and place on top of the vegetables. Pour over the stock and wine. Cover and cook in the oven at 180°C (350°F) mark 4 for 1 hour.

Remove the chicken, place on a heated serving dish, cover and keep warm. Bring the cooking liquid to the boil and boil rapidly until reduced by half. Remove from the heat and stir in the lightly beaten yogurt. Heat through for 1 minute without boiling and pour over the chicken. Garnish with watercress.
○ *Calories 419 (1701)*

Chicken and pepper risotto

600 ml (1 pint) chicken stock
175 g (6 oz) long grain rice
4 sticks of celery, washed and thinly sliced
25 g (1 oz) Flora
1 large onion, skinned and sliced
1 clove of garlic, skinned and crushed
1 green pepper, seeded and sliced
1 red pepper, seeded and sliced
225 g (8 oz) button mushrooms, sliced
salt and freshly ground black pepper
700 g (1½ lb) cooked chicken meat, diced
175 g (6 oz) sweetcorn kernels
30 ml (2 tbsp) chopped fresh rosemary
15 g (½ oz) flaked almonds, toasted,
to garnish

Bring the chicken stock to the boil in a large saucepan. Add the rice and celery, cover and cook for 15 minutes.

Melt the margarine in a frying pan and fry the onion and garlic for 2 minutes. Add the peppers, mushrooms and seasoning, and cook for a further 2 minutes. Stir the pepper mixture into the rice with the chicken and sweetcorn. Cover and cook gently for 15 minutes, stirring occasionally. Stir in the rosemary, spoon into a warm serving dish and scatter the almonds over the top to garnish.
○ *Calories 409 (1684)*

Chicken and sweetcorn flan

225 g (8 oz) all-in-one shortcrust pastry (see page 100)
25 g (1 oz) Flora
30 ml (2 level tbsp) flour
150 ml (¼ pint) skimmed milk
5 ml (1 level tsp) salt
15 ml (1 level tbsp) paprika
5 ml (1 level tsp) dry mustard
150 ml (¼ pint) low fat natural yogurt
100 g (4 oz) Edam cheese, grated
550 g (1¼ lb) cooked chicken meat, cubed
198-g (7-oz) can sweetcorn and peppers

Roll out the pastry dough and use to line a 21·5-cm (8½-in) flan ring. Melt the margarine in a saucepan, stir in the flour and cook for 2 minutes. Gradually stir in the milk, bring to the boil and cook for 2 minutes. Stir in the seasoning, yogurt, 75 g (3 oz) of the grated cheese, the chicken and sweetcorn. Pour into the pastry case, level the top and sprinkle with the remaining cheese. Bake in the oven at 190°C (375°F) mark 5 for 40–45 minutes until the filling is firm and golden brown. Serve hot or cold with a fresh mixed salad.
◑ *Calories 709 (2800)*

Garlic chicken with lemon sauce

4 225-g (8-oz) chicken breast portions, skinned and boned
1 lemon, sliced
300 ml (½ pint) chicken stock
15 g (½ oz) Flora
15 g (½ oz) flour
juice of 1 lemon
lemon slices and watercress to garnish

For the stuffing
100 g (4 oz) curd cheese
2 cloves of garlic, skinned and crushed
15 ml (1 tbsp) chopped fresh thyme
15 ml (1 tbsp) chopped fresh rosemary
salt and freshly ground black pepper

Mix the stuffing ingredients together in a bowl. Place the chicken breasts between sheets of greaseproof paper and flatten with a meat mallet or rolling pin. Spread the stuffing over the chicken breasts, roll up and secure with wooden cocktail sticks.

Place four slices of lemon in the bottom of an ovenproof dish. Place a chicken breast on each, pour over the stock and cover with foil. Cook in the oven at 180°C (350°F) mark 4 for 55 minutes. Uncover the chicken for the last 15 minutes to brown.

Place the chicken on a heated serving dish and keep warm. Reserve the stock but not the lemon slices. Melt the margarine in a saucepan, add the flour and cook for 2 minutes. Stir in 300 ml ($\frac{1}{2}$ pint) of the stock, bring to the boil and stir until thickened. Add the lemon juice and adjust the seasoning. Pour the sauce over the chicken and garnish with fresh lemon slices and watercress.

○ *Calories 352 (1408)*

Chicken and pineapple casserole

4 225-g (8-oz) chicken portions, skinned
45 ml (3 level tbsp) seasoned flour
25 g (1 oz) Flora
10 ml (2 tsp) sunflower oil
1 large onion, skinned and sliced
1 green pepper, seeded and sliced
150 ml ($\frac{1}{4}$ pint) chicken stock
300 ml ($\frac{1}{2}$ pint) white wine
salt and freshly ground white pepper
100 g (4 oz) button mushrooms
227-g (8-oz) can pineapple pieces, drained
watercress to garnish

Coat the chicken portions in seasoned flour. Heat the margarine and oil in a frying pan and fry the chicken for 10 minutes until brown. Place in an ovenproof casserole.

Fry the onion and pepper in the pan for 10 minutes. Add the stock and wine and bring to the boil, stirring. Pour over the chicken and season. Cover and cook in the oven at 180°C (350°F) mark 4 for 1 hour. Add the mushrooms and pineapple, recover and continue cooking for 15 minutes. Garnish with watercress.

○ *Calories 511 (2073)*

Turkey and grapefruit casserole

75 g (3 oz) dried apricots
4 225-g (8-oz) turkey breast portions, skinned
45 ml (3 level tbsp) seasoned flour
25 g (1 oz) Flora
1 medium onion, skinned and sliced
5 ml (1 level tsp) paprika
juice of 1 grapefruit
300 ml ($\frac{1}{2}$ pint) turkey or chicken stock
salt and freshly ground black pepper
5 ml (1 level tsp) caster sugar
1 grapefruit, peeled and segmented
watercress to garnish

Place the apricots in a small bowl, cover with boiling water and leave to soak for 1 hour until plump.

Coat the turkey portions with seasoned flour. Melt the margarine in a frying pan and fry the turkey portions for 3 minutes on each side until lightly browned. Place the turkey and the apricots in an ovenproof casserole.

Add the onion and paprika to the pan and fry gently for 15 minutes. Add any remaining seasoned flour to the pan and cook for 2 minutes. Stir in the grapefruit juice, stock, seasoning and sugar. Bring to the boil, stirring until thickened, and pour over the turkey. Cover and bake in the oven at 180°C (350°F) mark 4 for about $1\frac{1}{2}$ hours.

Remove the lid of the casserole, stir in the grapefruit segments and continue cooking for 5 minutes. Garnish with watercress.

○ *Calories 351 (1546)*

Turkey with ginger yogurt sauce

15 g ($\frac{1}{2}$ oz) Flora
4 225-g (8-oz) turkey breast portions, skinned
1 medium onion, skinned and sliced
400 ml ($\frac{3}{4}$ pint) turkey or chicken stock
2·5 ml ($\frac{1}{2}$ level tsp) ground ginger
5 ml (1 tsp) chopped fresh thyme
salt and freshly ground black pepper
15 ml (1 level tbsp) cornflour
45 ml (3 level tbsp) low fat natural yogurt
watercress to garnish

Melt the margarine in a flameproof casserole, add the turkey portions and fry for 3 minutes on each side until brown. Add the onion and fry gently for 5 minutes. Pour in the stock with the ground ginger, thyme and seasoning. Cover and cook in the oven at 180°C (350°F) mark 4 for about $1\frac{1}{2}$ hours until tender.

Remove the turkey portions to a heated serving dish, cover and keep warm. Blend the cornflour to a smooth paste with a little water and stir into the stock. Bring to the boil, stirring until thickened. Simmer gently for 3 minutes, then remove the pan from the heat. Lightly beat the yogurt, stir into the sauce and pour over the turkey. Garnish with watercress and serve with boiled rice.

○ *Calories 300 (1358)*

Chicken in plum sauce, served with courgettes

Chicken in plum sauce

Illustrated in colour on the cover

4 175-g (6-oz) chicken thigh portions, skinned
30 ml (2 level tbsp) seasoned flour
25 g (1 oz) Flora
2 medium onions, skinned and sliced
150 ml ($\frac{1}{4}$ pint) turkey or chicken stock
450 g (1 lb) golden plums, or 566-g $1\frac{1}{4}$-lb) can plums (drained), stoned and roughly chopped
30 ml (2 tbsp) ruby port
salt and freshly ground black pepper
chopped parsley or watercress to garnish

Coat the chicken portions in seasoned flour. Melt the margarine in a large frying pan, add the chicken portions and cook for 2 minutes on each side. Place in an ovenproof casserole. Add the onion to the pan and fry for 10 minutes until soft. Pour in the stock and boil for 2 minutes, stirring. Stir in the plums, port and seasoning and pour the sauce over the chicken. Cover and cook in the oven at 180°C (350°F) mark 4 for about $1\frac{1}{2}$ hours.

Remove the chicken portions to a heated serving dish. Pour a little of the plum sauce over the chicken and serve the remaining sauce separately. Garnish with parsley or watercress.

If liked, surround the chicken portions with boiled sliced courgettes to serve.

○ *Calories 300 (459)*

Rabbit braised with sherry

175 g (6 oz) mushrooms
15 g ($\frac{1}{2}$ oz) Flora
2 rashers lean bacon, rinded and chopped
225 g (8 oz) carrots, peeled and chopped
2 sticks of celery, washed and chopped
1 large onion, skinned and chopped
100 g (4 oz) turnip, peeled and chopped
1 clove of garlic, skinned and crushed
1-kg ($2\frac{1}{4}$-lb) rabbit, jointed
300 ml ($\frac{1}{2}$ pint) chicken stock
90 ml (6 tbsp) medium dry sherry
15 ml (1 level tbsp) tomato paste
salt and freshly ground pepper
5 ml (1 level tsp) dried mixed herbs
30 ml (2 level tbsp) cornflour

Chop the mushroom stalks finely and reserve the caps. Melt the margarine in a frying pan. Add the bacon, vegetables, mushroom stalks and garlic, fry for 10 minutes and place in an ovenproof casserole. Brown the rabbit pieces in the frying pan for 10 minutes until golden and transfer to the casserole. Add the stock, sherry, tomato paste, seasoning and herbs to the pan and bring to the boil. Pour over the rabbit, cover and cook in the oven at 180°C (350°F) mark 4 for 1½ hours until the rabbit is tender.

Remove the rabbit pieces from the casserole. Blend the cornflour to a smooth paste with a little water and stir into the casserole. Return the rabbit and add the mushroom caps. Cover and continue cooking for 15–20 minutes until thickened.

○ *Calories 380 (1513)*

Rabbit carbonade

60 ml (4 level tbsp) flour
15 ml (1 level tbsp) dry mustard
salt and freshly ground pepper
1-kg (2¼-lb) rabbit, jointed
25 g (1 oz) Flora
15 ml (1 tbsp) vegetable oil
3 sticks of celery, washed and chopped
225 g (8 oz) button onions, skinned
50 g (2 oz) sultanas
300 ml (½ pint) chicken stock
300 ml (½ pint) light ale

Stir the flour, mustard and seasoning together and toss the rabbit joints in the mixture until evenly coated. Heat the margarine and oil in a frying pan, add the celery and onions and fry for 5 minutes. Remove the vegetables from the pan with a slotted spoon and place in an ovenproof casserole. Add the rabbit pieces to the pan and fry for 10 minutes until golden brown. Place in the casserole with the vegetables and add the sultanas.

In the frying pan, cook any remaining seasoned flour for 1 minute. Gradually stir in the stock and ale. Bring to the boil, stirring, and pour into the casserole. Cover and cook in the oven at 180°C (350°F) mark 4 for about 1½ hours until the rabbit is tender.

○ *Calories 424 (1722)*

Sweet and sour rabbit casserole

15 g (½ oz) Flora
900-g (2-lb) rabbit, jointed
100 g (4 oz) lean bacon, rinded and diced
4 small onions, skinned and quartered
4 tomatoes, skinned, seeded and chopped
150 ml (¼ pint) dry cider
150 ml (¼ pint) chicken stock
30 ml (2 level tbsp) tomato paste
5 ml (1 level tsp) sugar
30 ml (2 tbsp) Worcestershire sauce
30 ml (2 level tbsp) mango chutney
salt and freshly ground black pepper
10 ml (2 level tsp) cornflour
chopped parsley to garnish

Melt the margarine in a flameproof casserole and fry the rabbit joints for 3 minutes until brown all over. Add the bacon and onions and fry for 5 minutes until golden brown. Add the tomatoes, cider, stock, tomato paste, sugar, Worcestershire sauce, chutney and seasoning. Stir well and bring to the boil. Cover and cook in the oven at 180°C (350°F) mark 4 for 1½ hours.

Remove the rabbit and onion to a heated serving dish, cover and keep warm. Blend the cornflour to a smooth paste with a little water and add to the cooking liquid. Bring to the boil, stirring until thickened. Adjust the seasoning, pour the sauce over the rabbit and sprinkle with the chopped parsley to garnish.

○ *Calories 425 (1717)*

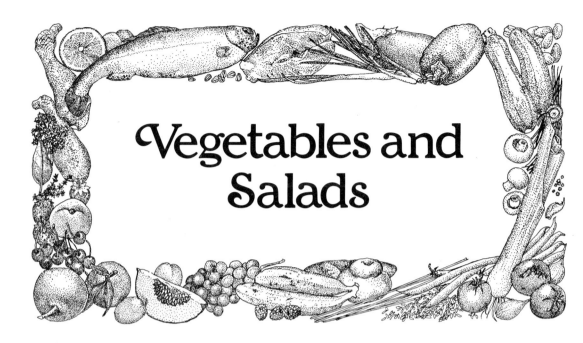

Vegetables and Salads

Spiced aubergines

700 g (1½ lb) aubergines, diced
salt
15 ml (1 tbsp) sunflower oil
1 medium onion, skinned and chopped
1 clove of garlic, skinned and crushed
2·5 ml (½ level tsp) ground coriander
2·5 ml (½ level tsp) turmeric
2·5 ml (½ level tsp) chilli powder
pinch of ground cardamom
2·5 ml (½ level tsp) salt
freshly ground black pepper
75 g (3 oz) button mushrooms, quartered
150 ml (¼ pint) chicken stock
75 ml (5 level tbsp) low fat natural yogurt
chopped parsley to garnish

Place the diced aubergine in a colander or
sieve, sprinkle with salt and leave for 30
minutes. Rinse off the salt under cold
running water and drain well.

Heat the oil in a large frying pan, add the
onion and garlic and fry gently for 10
minutes. Add the spices and seasoning and
fry for 2 minutes. Stir in the aubergine,
mushrooms and stock. Cover and simmer
gently for 15 minutes. Lightly beat the
yogurt, stir into the aubergine mixture and
heat gently without boiling. Spoon into a
heated serving dish and sprinkle with parsley.
○ Calories 83 (342)

Green beans and mushrooms in wine

Illustrated in colour facing page 64

25 g (1 oz) Flora
1 clove of garlic, skinned and crushed
1 small onion, skinned and finely chopped
700 g (1½ lb) French or runner beans,
    trimmed
100 g (4 oz) button mushrooms, sliced
150 ml (¼ pint) dry white wine
salt and freshly ground black pepper

Melt the margarine in a large saucepan,
add the garlic and onion and fry for 10
minutes. Add the beans and mushrooms
and fry gently for 3 minutes. Stir in the
wine and seasoning. Cover and simmer
gently for 10–15 minutes until the beans
are tender but still crisp. Spoon into a
heated serving dish.
○ Calories 101 (422)

Chilli carrots

15 g (½ oz) Flora
1 clove of garlic, skinned and crushed
1 medium onion, skinned and sliced
2·5 ml (½ level tsp) chilli seasoning
salt and freshly ground black pepper
900 g (2 lb) carrots, peeled and thinly sliced
1 red pepper, seeded and thinly sliced
150 ml (¼ pint) chicken stock
150 ml (¼ pint) low fat natural yogurt
chopped parsley to garnish

Melt the margarine in a large frying pan, add the garlic, onion and chilli seasoning and fry for 10 minutes. Add the salt and pepper, carrots, red pepper and stock. Cover and simmer gently for 10–15 minutes until the carrots are tender.

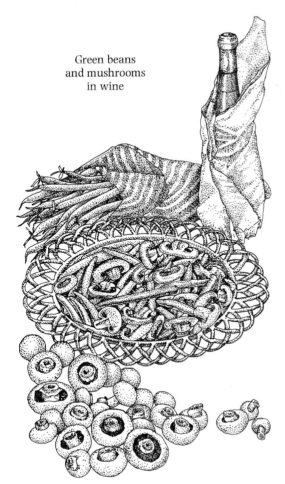

Green beans
and mushrooms
in wine

Remove from the heat, stir in the lightly beaten yogurt and reheat gently without boiling. Spoon into a heated serving dish and sprinkle with parsley.
○ *Calories 104 (426)*

Cauliflower coriander

900 g (2 lb) cauliflower, trimmed and divided
  into small florets
2·5 ml (½ level tsp) turmeric
40 g (1½ oz) Flora
15 g (½ oz) flour
2·5 ml (½ level tsp) ground coriander
300 ml (½ pint) skimmed milk
salt and freshly ground black pepper
25 g (1 oz) fresh brown breadcrumbs
15 ml (1 tbsp) chopped parsley

Cook the cauliflower in boiling salted water with the turmeric for 10–12 minutes.

Meanwhile, melt 15 g (½ oz) of the margarine in a saucepan, add the flour and coriander and cook for 3 minutes. Gradually add the milk, bring to the boil, stirring, and cook for 3 minutes. Add the seasoning. Melt the remaining margarine and fry the breadcrumbs for 3–4 minutes until crisp and golden; stir in the parsley. Drain the cauliflower well and arrange in a heated serving dish. Pour over the sauce and sprinkle with the breadcrumbs.
○ *Calories 161 (618)*

Cheesy cauliflower provençale

15 g (½ oz) Flora
1 large onion, skinned and chopped
1 clove of garlic, skinned and crushed
300 ml (½ pint) beef stock
450 g (1 lb) tomatoes, skinned and chopped
10 ml (2 level tsp) dried oregano
30 ml (2 level tbsp) tomato paste
5 ml (1 level tsp) caster sugar
salt and freshly ground black pepper
900 g (2 lb) cauliflower, trimmed and divided
  into florets
22·5 ml (1½ level tbsp) cornflour
6 black olives, halved and stoned
75 g (3 oz) mozzarella cheese, sliced

Melt the margarine in a large saucepan, add the onion and garlic, cover and fry gently for 15 minutes. Stir in the stock, tomatoes, oregano, tomato paste, sugar and seasoning. Cover and simmer gently for 20 minutes.

Meanwhile, cook the cauliflower florets in boiling salted water for 15 minutes. Drain thoroughly and place in a heated flameproof dish. Blend the cornflour to a smooth paste with a little water and add to the tomato sauce. Bring to the boil, stirring until thickened. Pour the sauce over the cauliflower and scatter with the olives. Lay the sliced cheese over the top and cook under a hot grill for about 5 minutes until the cheese melts and bubbles.
○ *Calories 182 (739)*

Carrot and parsnip croquettes

450 g (1 lb) carrots, peeled and sliced
450 g (1 lb) parsnips, peeled and diced
salt and freshly ground black pepper
60 ml (4 tbsp) chopped parsley
1·25 ml (¼ level tsp) grated nutmeg
50 g (2 oz) fresh white breadcrumbs
40 g (1½ oz) Flora
10 ml (2 tsp) sunflower oil

Cook the carrots and parsnips in boiling salted water for 25 minutes until very tender. Drain well and mash. Stir in the seasoning, parsley and nutmeg and chill for

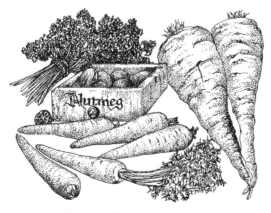
Carrot and parsnip croquettes

about 1 hour. Divide the mixture into eight, shape into croquettes using a palette knife and coat with the breadcrumbs.

Heat the margarine and oil in a large frying pan and fry the croquettes gently for 10 minutes until golden brown all over. Drain on kitchen paper towel.
○ *Calories 224 (878)*

Courgettes portugaise

25 g (1 oz) Flora
1 large onion, skinned and chopped
1 clove of garlic, skinned and crushed
10 ml (2 level tsp) paprika
15 ml (1 level tbsp) tomato paste
1·25 ml (¼ level tsp) grated nutmeg
salt and freshly ground pepper
25 g (1 oz) flour
300 ml (½ pint) chicken stock
4 tomatoes, skinned, seeded and chopped
900 g (2 lb) courgettes, sliced

Melt the margarine in a large saucepan, add the onion and garlic and fry for 10 minutes. Stir in the paprika, tomato paste, nutmeg, seasoning and flour and cook for 2 minutes, stirring. Gradually stir in the stock with the tomatoes. Bring to the boil and simmer the sauce gently for 15 minutes until it becomes a thick purée.

Cook the courgettes in boiling salted water for 5 minutes. Drain thoroughly, stir into the spiced purée and reheat. Turn into a heated serving dish.
○ *Calories 117 (447)*

Golden garlic creamed potatoes

900 g (2 lb) potatoes, peeled and quartered
2 cloves of garlic, skinned and crushed
25 g (1 oz) Flora
salt and freshly ground black pepper
1·25 ml (¼ level tsp) grated nutmeg
30 ml (2 tbsp) chopped parsley
150 ml (¼ pint) skimmed milk
1 egg white, beaten

Place the potatoes in a saucepan of salted water, cover, bring to the boil and cook for

20 minutes. Drain well. Mash the potatoes until smooth. Add the garlic, margarine, seasoning, nutmeg, parsley and milk and mix well. Spoon into a heated flameproof dish, level the top and mark with a fork. Brush with the egg white and brown under a hot grill for about 5 minutes. *Serves 6*
○ *Calories 256 (1028)*

Herby potatoes

900 g (2 lb) potatoes, peeled and diced
large sprig of mint
300 ml ($\frac{1}{2}$ pint) low fat natural yogurt
30 ml (2 tbsp) chopped fresh mint
30 ml (2 tbsp) chopped parsley
30 ml (2 tbsp) chopped fresh chives
5 ml (1 level tsp) caster sugar
salt and freshly ground black pepper
parsley sprigs to garnish

Place the potatoes in a pan of salted water with a sprig of mint. Cover, bring to the boil and cook for 15 minutes.

Meanwhile, lightly beat the yogurt in a bowl and stir in the herbs, sugar and seasoning. Drain the potatoes well and return to the pan. Add the yogurt dressing to the potatoes and heat gently without boiling. Spoon into a heated serving dish and garnish with sprigs of parsley. *Serves 6*
○ *Calories 223 (915)*

Cheesy stuffed tomatoes

8 large tomatoes
15 g ($\frac{1}{2}$ oz) Flora
1 large onion, skinned and grated
2 cloves of garlic, skinned and crushed
salt and freshly ground black pepper
15 ml (1 tbsp) chopped fresh thyme
30 ml (2 tbsp) chopped parsley
75 g (3 oz) dry brown breadcrumbs
50 g (2 oz) Edam cheese, grated
2·5 ml ($\frac{1}{2}$ tsp) sunflower oil
watercress to garnish

Cut the tops off the tomatoes, scoop out the pulp and retain. Melt the margarine in a frying pan, add the onion and garlic and fry gently for 4 minutes. Add the tomato pulp and season well. Stir over a high heat for 10 minutes until the mixture becomes a thick purée. Stir in the herbs, breadcrumbs and half the cheese.

Spoon the stuffing into the tomatoes and sprinkle the remaining cheese over the top. Brush the bottom of an ovenproof dish and the sides of the tomatoes with the oil. Place the tomatoes in the dish and bake in the oven at 180°C (350°F) mark 4 for 25 minutes. Serve garnished with watercress.
○ *Calories 161 (597)*

Crispy stir-fried vegetables

15 ml (1 tbsp) sunflower oil
1 medium onion, skinned and thinly sliced
450 g (1 lb) celery, washed and thinly sliced
1 large green pepper, seeded and thinly sliced
100 g (4 oz) fresh bean sprouts
30 ml (2 tbsp) Worcestershire sauce
5 ml (1 level tsp) salt
freshly ground black pepper

Heat the oil in a large frying pan and add the vegetables. Stir the vegetables well to coat them with the hot oil and fry for 1 minute, stirring. Add the Worcestershire sauce and seasoning and continue stirring and frying for 5 minutes. Spoon into a heated serving dish and serve immediately.
○ *Calories 58 (242)*

Chilled fennel salad

450 g (1 lb) fennel, trimmed and thinly sliced
100 g (4 oz) button mushrooms, sliced
chopped fresh chives to garnish

For the dressing
30 ml (2 tbsp) wine vinegar
60 ml (4 tbsp) sunflower oil
salt and freshly ground black pepper
2·5 ml ($\frac{1}{2}$ level tsp) grated nutmeg
2·5 ml ($\frac{1}{2}$ level tsp) made mustard

Blanch the fennel in boiling salted water for 5 minutes, then drain and plunge into cold water. Whisk together the dressing ingredients and pour over the fennel while

still warm. Stir in the mushrooms and spoon into a serving dish. Cover and chill overnight. Serve sprinkled with chives.
○ *Calories 140 (572)*

Beetroot salad with walnut dressing

450 g (1 lb) beetroot, cooked and skinned
2 oranges, peeled and segmented
chopped parsley to garnish

For the dressing
15 ml (1 tbsp) wine vinegar
30 ml (2 tbsp) sunflower oil
salt and freshly ground black pepper
1·25 ml (¼ level tsp) made mustard
50 g (2 oz) walnuts, finely chopped

Cut the beetroot into 1-cm (½-in) cubes and place in a large mixing bowl. Cut each orange segment in half and add to the beetroot with any of the juice.

For the dressing, whisk together the vinegar, oil, seasoning and mustard. Stir in the walnuts. Pour over the salad and toss well. Cover and chill for 30 minutes. Spoon into a serving dish and sprinkle with parsley.
○ *Calories 212 (836)*

Green pepper and cucumber salad

1 cucumber, peeled and diced
salt
2 green peppers, halved and seeded
4 sticks of celery, washed and sliced
25 g (1 oz) sultanas
grated rind of ½ lemon

For the dressing
30 ml (2 tbsp) lemon juice
30 ml (2 tbsp) wine vinegar
60 ml (4 tbsp) sunflower oil
salt and freshly ground black pepper
1·25 ml (¼ level tsp) made mustard

Place the cucumber in a colander, sprinkle with salt and leave for 30 minutes. Rinse under running water, drain and pat dry

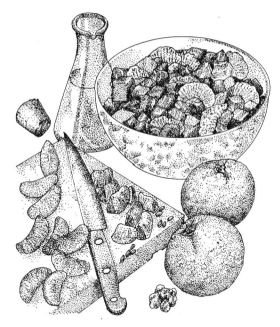
Beetroot salad with walnut dressing

with kitchen paper towel. Meanwhile, put the peppers under a hot grill for a few minutes until the skin blisters. Plunge into cold water and drain. Peel off the skin and slice into 0·5-cm (¼-in) strips.

Mix together the cucumber, pepper, celery, sultanas and lemon rind. Whisk together the dressing ingredients, pour over the salad and toss well. Spoon into a serving dish and chill for 30 minutes.
○ *Calories 183 (752)*

Leek and mushroom salad

2 medium leeks, trimmed, thinly sliced and washed
75 g (3 oz) button mushrooms, sliced
45 ml (3 tbsp) chopped fresh chives

For the dressing
30 ml (2 tbsp) wine vinegar
60 ml (4 tbsp) sunflower oil
1·25 ml (¼ level tsp) made mustard
salt and freshly ground black pepper
30 ml (2 tbsp) lemon juice

Blanch the leeks in boiling salted water for

2 minutes. Drain. Combine the leeks, mushrooms and chives in a mixing bowl. Whisk together the dressing ingredients and pour over the salad. Toss well and spoon into a serving dish. Cover and chill overnight.
○ *Calories 145 (597)*

Lemon dressed corn salad

225 g (8 oz) long grain rice
175 g (6 oz) sweetcorn kernels
1 lemon
small bunch fresh tarragon
4 black olives

For the dressing
15 ml (1 tbsp) wine vinegar
30 ml (2 tbsp) sunflower oil
salt and freshly ground black pepper
1·25 ml (¼ level tsp) made mustard

Cook the rice and sweetcorn in a saucepan of boiling salted water for 12–15 minutes, with a slice of lemon and sprig of tarragon. Drain and rinse under cold running water; remove the tarragon and lemon.

Place the rice and sweetcorn in a large bowl and add the grated rind of the remaining lemon and 45 ml (3 tbsp) juice. Whisk together the dressing ingredients and pour over the salad with 30 ml (2 tbsp) chopped tarragon. Toss well and spoon into a serving dish. Scatter the olives over the top and chill for about 30 minutes before serving.
○ *Calories 195 (836)*

Pasta and tomato salad

100 g (4 oz) pasta shells
175 g (6 oz) sweetcorn kernels
4 sticks of celery, washed and sliced
4 tomatoes, skinned, quartered and seeded
chopped parsley to garnish

For the dressing
150 ml (¼ pint) low fat natural yogurt
60 ml (4 tbsp) tomato juice
1·25 ml (¼ tsp) Worcestershire sauce
salt and freshly ground black pepper
10 ml (2 tsp) chopped fresh oregano

Cook the pasta shells and sweetcorn in boiling salted water for 12–15 minutes. Drain and rinse under running cold water. Combine with the celery and tomatoes in a large mixing bowl.

Mix the dressing ingredients together, pour over the salad and toss well. Spoon into a serving dish, sprinkle with parsley, cover and chill for about 30 minutes before serving.
○ *Calories 103 (397)*

Chinese vegetable salad

225 g (8 oz) Chinese leaves, finely shredded
100 g (4 oz) fennel, thinly sliced
100 g (4 oz) carrots, peeled and grated
50 g (2 oz) sultanas
2 red eating apples, cored and sliced
30 ml (2 tbsp) lemon juice
300 ml (½ pint) low fat natural yogurt
5 ml (1 level tsp) Dijon mustard
chopped fresh chives to garnish

Place the Chinese leaves, fennel, carrots and sultanas in a large mixing bowl. Toss the apples in the lemon juice and stir into the Chinese leaves.

Lightly beat together the yogurt and mustard, pour over the salad and mix well until the vegetables are evenly coated. Spoon into a serving dish and chill for about 30 minutes before serving. Garnish with chives.
○ *Calories 110 (415)*

Sweetcorn, rice and cheese salad

175 g (6 oz) long grain rice
100 g (4 oz) sweetcorn kernels, cooked
100 g (4 oz) peas, cooked
225 g (8 oz) Edam cheese, diced
1 curly endive, trimmed and washed

For the dressing
30 ml (2 tbsp) wine vinegar
60 ml (4 tbsp) sunflower oil
2·5 ml ($\frac{1}{2}$ level tsp) made mustard
salt and freshly ground black pepper

Cook the rice in boiling salted water for 15 minutes until tender and drain. Whisk together the dressing ingredients and pour over the rice while still warm. Stir well until evenly coated then leave to cool. Stir in the sweetcorn, peas and cheese. Arrange the endive in a shallow serving dish, pile the rice mixture on top and chill for 15 minutes before serving.

◗ *Calories 403 (1668)*

Avocado and tomato rice salad

175 g (6 oz) long grain rice
4 tomatoes, skinned, quartered and seeded
8 large spring onions, trimmed and sliced
2 large ripe avocados
juice of 1 lemon
30 ml (2 tbsp) chopped fresh mint

For the dressing
30 ml (2 tbsp) wine vinegar
60 ml (4 tbsp) sunflower oil
1·25 ml ($\frac{1}{4}$ level tsp) made mustard
salt and freshly ground black pepper

Cook the rice in boiling salted water for 12–15 minutes, drain and place in a large bowl. Whisk together the dressing ingredients and pour over the rice while still warm. Toss well and leave to cool.

Add the tomatoes and onions. Peel, stone and dice the avocados, toss in the lemon juice and stir into the rice salad with the chopped mint. Spoon into a serving dish and chill for 30 minutes before serving.

○ *Calories 262 (1103)*

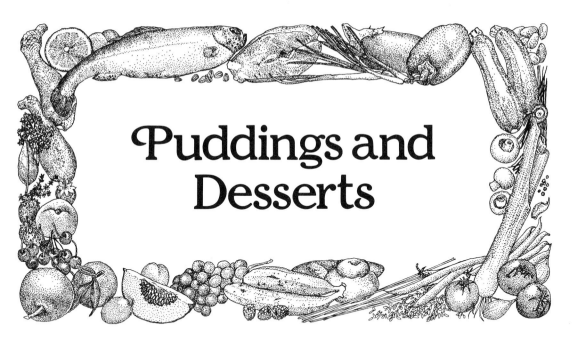

Puddings and Desserts

South Sea oranges

4 large oranges, peeled
90 ml (6 level tbsp) icing sugar, sifted
100 g (4 oz) grated fresh coconut or
   desiccated coconut
45 ml (3 tbsp) orange juice

Cut across the orange segments into
0·25-cm ($\frac{1}{8}$-in) slices. Layer one third of the
slices in a serving dish. Sprinkle with 30 ml
(2 level tbsp) of the sugar, one third of the
coconut and 15 ml (1 tbsp) of the orange
juice. Repeat this layering twice with the
remaining ingredients and chill thoroughly.
○ *Calories 285 (1168)*

Melon fruit cups

2 Charentais melons, halved and seeded
5 ml (1 level tsp) grated lemon rind
10 ml (2 level tsp) grated orange rind
30 ml (2 tbsp) lemon juice
175 ml (6 fl oz) orange juice
50 g (2 oz) sugar
fresh mint sprigs to decorate

Scoop the flesh from the melons with a
melon baller or cut into cubes. Reserve the
skins. In a small saucepan mix the lemon

and orange rind and juices and the sugar.
Bring to the boil, stirring until the sugar has
dissolved. Reduce the heat and simmer
uncovered for 5 minutes. Cool the syrup
then chill for at least 2 hours. Toss the
melon in the syrup and pile back into the
reserved half shells. Garnish with mint.
○ *Calories 176 (710)*

Plum Betty

450 g (1 lb) plums, halved and stoned
100 g (4 oz) soft brown sugar
45 ml (3 tbsp) water
4 thick slices of wholemeal bread
30 ml (2 level tbsp) thick honey
25 g (1 oz) Flora

Place the plums, sugar and water in a
saucepan. Bring to the boil slowly, reduce
the heat and simmer gently for 15–20
minutes until soft. Allow to cool.

Cut the bread into 2-cm ($\frac{3}{4}$-in) cubes.
Layer half the plums in the bottom of a
1·2-litre (2-pint) ovenproof dish. Cover
with half the bread. Repeat with the remaining plums and bread. Drizzle the
honey all over the bread and dot with the

margarine. Bake in the oven at 190°C (375°F) mark 5 for about 1 hour until the bread is crisp and golden.

○ *Calories 313 (1315)*

Glazed lemon tart

Illustrated in colour facing page 65

175 g (6 oz) all-in-one shortcrust pastry (see page 100)

For the filling
30 ml (2 level tbsp) lemon curd
50 g (2 oz) Flora
50 g (2 oz) caster sugar
1 egg
grated rind of 1 lemon
50 g (2 oz) ground almonds
25 g (1 oz) plain white flour
2·5 ml ($\frac{1}{2}$ level tsp) baking powder
100 g (4 oz) granulated sugar
150 ml ($\frac{1}{4}$ pint) water
2 lemons, thinly sliced

Roll out the pastry dough and use to line a 20·5-cm (8-in) plain flan ring. Spread the bottom of the pastry case with the lemon curd. In a mixing bowl beat together the margarine, sugar, egg, lemon rind, almonds, flour and baking powder for 2–3 minutes, then spread this mixture over the lemon curd. Bake in the oven at 180°C (350°F) mark 4 for 35–40 minutes until the filling is risen and firm to the touch.

Dissolve the granulated sugar in the water in a small saucepan and add the lemon slices. Cook for 5–10 minutes until tender, then remove from the pan and reserve. Bring the syrup to the boil and boil vigorously until reduced by half to a thick glaze. Arrange the lemon slices over the tart and brush with the glaze. *Serves 4–6*

◑ *Calories 749 (2797) for 4*
499 (1865) for 6

Orange yogurt flan

175 g (6 oz) all-in-one shortcrust pastry (see page 100)
225 g (8 oz) cottage cheese
150 ml ($\frac{1}{4}$ pint) low fat natural yogurt
2 oranges
30 ml (2 level tbsp) demerara sugar

Roll out the pastry dough and use to line an 18-cm (7-inch) fluted flan case. Bake blind in the oven at 200°C (400°F) mark 6 for 10–15 minutes. Cool.

Mix together the cottage cheese, yogurt and grated orange rind. Remove the pith from the oranges with a sharp knife and slice the oranges thinly. Spoon the cottage cheese and yogurt mixture into the cooled flan case and arrange the orange slices, overlapping, around the edge. Sprinkle over the demerara sugar. Bake in the oven at 200°C (400°F) mark 6 for 30–35 minutes. Serve chilled. *Serves 4–6*

○ *Calories 452 (1646) for 4*
301 (1096) for 6

Crispy baked rhubarb

225 g (8 oz) rhubarb, cut into 1-cm ($\frac{1}{2}$-in) lengths
100 g (4 oz) granulated sugar
2·5 ml ($\frac{1}{2}$ level tsp) ground cinnamon

For the topping
25 g (1 oz) Flora
50 g (2 oz) plain white flour
25 g (1 oz) rolled oats
50 g (2 oz) light brown sugar

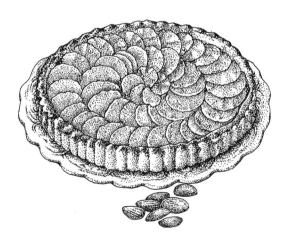

Glazed lemon tart

Place the rhubarb in an ovenproof pie dish and sprinkle with the sugar and cinnamon.

For the topping, rub the margarine into the flour and stir in the oats and sugar. Sprinkle the topping over the rhubarb and bake in the oven at 180°C (350°F) mark 4 for 40–45 minutes until the topping is golden brown and the rhubarb tender.
○ *Calories 303 (1189)*

Apples poached in cider

50 g (2 oz) Flora
2 large cooking apples, peeled, cored and
  sliced
25 g (1 oz) arrowroot
25 g (1 oz) demerara sugar
5 ml (1 level tsp) ground cinnamon
400 ml (¾ pint) dry cider

Melt the margarine in a large saucepan and toss the apples in it carefully, coating each slice. Place in an ovenproof dish. Mix together the arrowroot, sugar and cinnamon and sprinkle over the apples. Pour over the cider and bake in the oven at 160°C (325°F) mark 3 for 30–40 minutes until the apple slices are tender. Drain the liquid from the apples and boil quickly until reduced to a coating consistency. Pour the syrup over the apple slices and chill thoroughly. Serve with low fat natural yogurt.
○ *Calories 228 (924)*

Blackcurrant sorbet

300 ml (½ pint) water
100 g (4 oz) sugar
225 g (8 oz) blackcurrants, topped and tailed
5 ml (1 tsp) lemon juice
2 egg whites

Heat the water and sugar together in a saucepan, stirring until the sugar has dissolved. Bring to the boil and simmer gently for 10 minutes. Cool. Meanwhile, simmer the blackcurrants in a little water for 10 minutes until tender. Rub through a sieve and if necessary make up the purée to

Blackcurrant sorbet

300 ml (½ pint) with water. Cool, add the lemon juice and sugar syrup and pour into an ice tray. Freeze for about 1 hour until nearly firm.

Whisk the egg whites until stiff. Turn the half-frozen mixture into a chilled bowl and whisk until smooth. Fold in the egg whites, return to the ice tray and freeze until firm. Spoon into glass serving dishes.

To make strawberry or raspberry sorbet
Follow the same method, but do not cook the fruit. Simply rub the raw fruit through a sieve to make a purée and make up to 300 ml (½ pint) with water. *Serves 4–6*
○ *Calories 137 (622 for 4*
       91 (416) for 6

Apricot water ice

400 ml (¾ pint) water
100 g (4 oz) sugar
juice of 2 lemons
450 g (1 lb) apricot jam
1 egg white

Heat the water and sugar together in a saucepan, stirring until the sugar has dissolved. Bring to the boil and simmer for 10 minutes. Stir in the lemon juice and jam. Purée in a blender or rub through a sieve.

Pour into ice trays or plastic containers and freeze until mushy but not firm. Beat well, then fold in the stiffly whisked egg white. Return to the ice trays; freeze until set; spoon into individual dishes. *Serves 8*
○ *Calories 209 (903)*

Baked mango and honey apples

Baked mango and honey apples

4 large cooking apples, cored
60 ml (4 level tbsp) mango chutney
60 ml (4 level tbsp) honey
100 g (4 oz) Flora
25 g (1 oz) walnuts, chopped, to decorate

With a sharp knife gently cut through the skin around the circumference of each apple and place in an ovenproof dish. Fill each apple with 15 ml (1 level tbsp) chutney and 15 ml (1 level tbsp) honey and top with a 25 g (1 oz) knob of margarine. Cover with foil and bake in the oven at 190°C (375°F) mark 5 for 35–40 minutes until tender, basting the apples from time to time. Before serving, sprinkle with the walnuts.
○ *Calories 489 (2037)*

Blackberry shortcake

For the shortcake
450 g (1 lb) plain white flour
15 ml (1 level tbsp) baking powder
2·5 ml (½ level tsp) salt
100 g (4 oz) Flora
50 g (2 oz) granulated sugar
200 ml (⅓ pint) skimmed milk

For the topping
900 g (2 lb) blackberries
175 g (6 oz) granulated sugar
30 ml (2 level tbsp) icing sugar, sifted

For the shortcake, sift the flour, baking powder and salt into a bowl. Rub in the margarine and stir in the sugar. Add the milk all at once and mix to a firm dough with a fork. Spoon into a 20·5-cm (8-in)

square greased cake tin. Bake in the oven at 220°C (450°F) mark 8 for 12–15 minutes until golden.

Crush 700 g (1½ lb) of the blackberries with a potato masher. Add the sugar and remaining whole berries. Split the shortcake in half and use half the blackberry mixture to sandwich it together. Pile the remaining blackberries on top and dredge the cake with the icing sugar. *Serves 4–6*
○ *Calories 918 (3893) for 4*
612 (2596) for 6

Quick strawberry cheesecake

Illustrated in colour facing page 65

For the biscuit crust
175 g (6 oz) digestive biscuits, crushed
75 g (3 oz) Flora, melted

For the filling
1 packet strawberry jelly
225 g (8 oz) cottage cheese, sieved
50 g (2 oz) caster sugar

For the topping
175 g (6 oz) fresh, frozen or canned strawberries
150 ml (¼ pint) strawberry yogurt

Stir the crushed biscuits into the margarine and press into the bottom of a 20·5-cm (8-in) flan ring placed on a serving plate. Chill well.

In a measuring jug, dissolve the jelly in hot water so that it makes 150 ml ($\frac{1}{4}$ pint). Allow to cool. Beat together the sieved cottage cheese and caster sugar and gradually beat in the jelly. Spoon the filling into the biscuit crust and chill until set.

Carefully remove the flan ring, swirl a little yogurt on top and decorate with strawberries. Serve with the remaining yogurt. *Serves 4–6*

◑ *Calories 606 (2663) for 4*
           404 (1777) for 6

Raspberry pavlova

3 egg whites
175 g (6 oz) soft brown sugar
2·5 ml ($\frac{1}{2}$ tsp) vanilla essence
15 ml (1 tbsp) vinegar
5 ml (1 level tsp) cornflour
225 g (8 oz) curd cheese
sugar to taste
100 g (4 oz) fresh or frozen raspberries

Draw an 18-cm (7-in) circle on non-stick paper on a baking sheet. Whisk the egg whites until very stiff, then gradually whisk in the sugar. Fold in the vanilla essence, vinegar and cornflour. Spoon the meringue mixture on to the circle and shape into a round. Bake in the oven at 150°C (300°F) mark 2 for 1 hour until firm. Leave to cool.

Invert the Pavlova on to a serving plate and carefully remove the non-stick paper. Mix the curd cheese with a little sugar until smooth and pile on top of the meringue. Decorate with the raspberries.

◑ *Calories 324 (1210)*

Coffee froth delight

30 ml (2 level tbsp) powdered gelatine
generous 400 ml ($\frac{3}{4}$ pint) water
30 ml (2 level tbsp) instant coffee powder
225 g (8 oz) skimmed milk powder
few drops of almond essence
30 ml (2 level tbsp) sugar
grated chocolate to decorate

Place the gelatine and 60 ml (4 tbsp) of the water in a small heatproof bowl. Stand in a saucepan of hot water and allow to dissolve. While still warm, stir in the instant coffee. In a mixing bowl dissolve half the milk powder in 200 ml ($\frac{1}{3}$ pint) of the water. Beat in the gelatine and coffee liquid, almond essence and sugar. Refrigerate for about 30 minutes until the mixture has thickened to the consistency of unbeaten egg white.

Meanwhile, whisk the rest of the milk powder with the remaining 150 ml ($\frac{1}{4}$ pint) cold water until stiff peaks form when the beater is raised. Fold into the coffee mixture until well combined. Spoon into six individual glass dishes. Chill and decorate the coffee desserts with grated chocolate. *Serves 6*

○ *Calories 179 (727)*

Loganberry and apple walnut crumble

For the filling
225 g (8 oz) loganberries
225 g (8 oz) cooking apples, peeled, cored and sliced
25 g (1 oz) sugar
30 ml (2 tbsp) water

For the topping
100 g (4 oz) wholemeal flour
1·25 ml ($\frac{1}{4}$ level tsp) ground ginger
50 g (2 oz) Flora
25 g (1 oz) walnuts, finely chopped
50 g (2 oz) demerara sugar

Place the fruit for the filling in a greased 1·2-litre (2-pint) pie dish and sprinkle with the sugar and water. For the topping, stir the flour and ginger together in a mixing bowl and rub in the margarine until the mixture resembles fine breadcrumbs. Stir in the walnuts and sugar. Spoon the crumble mixture over the fruit and bake in the oven at 180°C (350°F) mark 4 for 25–30 minutes until golden brown.

○ *Calories 352 (1399)*

Chocolate and orange mousse

Spicy bread pudding

225 g (8 oz) stale white bread, crusts removed
300 ml (½ pint) skimmed milk
50 g (2 oz) chopped mixed peel
100 g (4 oz) currants
50 g (2 oz) sultanas
75 g (3 oz) Flora
50 g (2 oz) demerara sugar
grated rind of 1 orange
grated rind of 1 lemon
20 ml (4 level tsp) mixed spice
1 egg
grated nutmeg and caster sugar to serve

Crumble the bread into small pieces in a mixing bowl. Pour over the milk and leave to soak for 20 minutes. Add the remaining ingredients and beat well to give a soft dropping consistency.

Pour into a greased 1·2-litre (2-pint) pie dish and bake in the oven at 180°C (350°F) mark 4 for 1¾–2 hours until golden brown.

Serve hot or cold, sprinkled with nutmeg and sugar.
◖ *Calories 554 (2200)*

Chocolate and orange mousse

30 ml (2 level tbsp) cornflour
400 ml (¾ pint) skimmed milk
100 g (4 oz) caster sugar
30 ml (2 level tbsp) cocoa powder
grated rind of 1 orange
4 egg whites
blanched orange rind strips to decorate

In a small bowl blend the cornflour to a smooth paste with 60 ml (4 tbsp) of the skimmed milk. Place the remaining milk and the sugar, cocoa and grated orange rind in a large saucepan and stir while bringing to the boil. Pour on to the cornflour mixture, stirring. Return to the saucepan and bring back to the boil, stirring until thickened. Pour into a glass bowl, sprinkle with a little sugar to prevent a skin forming and leave until cold.

Beat the cold chocolate mixture with a wooden spoon, adding a little more skimmed milk if it is too stiff. Whisk the egg whites until stiff and glossy. Fold into the chocolate mixture with a metal spoon. Pour into a glass bowl or individual serving dishes and chill thoroughly before serving. Decorate with orange rind. *Serves 6*
○ *Calories 140 (617)*

Apple and grapefruit whip

450 g (1 lb) cooking apples, peeled, cored and
   sliced
75 ml (5 tbsp) water
30 ml (2 level tbsp) powdered gelatine
100 g (4 oz) caster sugar
grated rind and juice of 1 large grapefruit
150 ml (¼ pint) low fat natural yogurt
3 egg whites
chopped walnuts to decorate

Cook the apples in a saucepan with 15 ml (1 tbsp) of the water until soft, then purée in a blender or rub through a sieve.

Place the gelatine in a small heatproof bowl, add the remaining water and stand the bowl in a pan of hot water until the gelatine dissolves. In a large basin, mix together the apple purée, sugar, grapefruit rind and juice and yogurt. Stir in the dissolved gelatine. Leave in the refrigerator until partially set.

Whisk the egg whites until stiff and fold them into the fruit mixture. Pour into a glass serving dish and allow to set completely. Decorate with chopped walnuts.

○ *Calories 242 (1067)*

Baked butterscotch peaches

425-g (15-oz) can peach halves, drained
50 g (2 oz) Flora
50 g (2 oz) soft brown sugar
25 g (1 oz) walnuts, chopped

Place the peach halves in an ovenproof dish. Cream the margarine and sugar until fluffy and stir in the chopped walnuts. Spoon over the peaches. Bake in the oven at 200°C (400°F) mark 6 for 25–30 minutes until the topping is crispy.

○ *Calories 252 (978)*

Baking

All-in-one shortcrust pastry

175-g (6-oz) quantity
100 g (3½ oz) Flora
15 ml (1 tbsp) water
175 g (6 oz) plain flour, sifted

225-g (8-oz) quantity
150 g (5 oz) Flora
15–22 ml (1–1½ tbsp) water
225 g (8 oz) plain flour, sifted

Place the margarine, water and one third of the flour in a mixing bowl and cream with a fork until well mixed.

Stir in the remaining flour to form a firm dough, turn on to a lightly floured surface and knead until smooth.

Roll out the pastry in the normal way and use as required.

○ *Calories   1410 (6090) for 175-g (6-oz) recipe*
1890 (8127) for 225-g (8-oz) recipe

Hints for making successful All-in-one shortcrust pastry
1 Use margarine straight from the refrigerator or cool larder. If allowed to become soft before using, the pastry may be sticky and not easy to handle.

2 Mix the margarine, water and one third of the flour together only until *just* mixed, particularly if the margarine has become rather soft.

3 Mix in the remaining flour and knead very thoroughly until smooth. Unlike rubbed-in pastry, this kneading will not toughen pastry but improve it.

4 Chill the pastry before using.

All-in-one wholemeal pastry

150 g (5 oz) Flora
15–22 ml (1–1½ tbsp) water
100 g (4 oz) plain white flour
100 g (4 oz) wholemeal flour

Place the margarine, water and the white flour in a mixing bowl and cream with a fork until well mixed.

Stir in the remaining flour to form a firm dough, turn on to a lightly floured surface and knead until smooth. Roll out and use as required.

○ *Calories 1826 (6070), whole recipe*

Wholemeal bread

700 g (1½ lb) wholemeal flour
225 g (8 oz) plain white flour
10 ml (2 level tsp) salt
25 g (1 oz) Flora
25 g (1 oz) fresh yeast
5 ml (1 level tsp) caster sugar
600 ml (1 pint) tepid water

Stir the flours and salt together in a mixing bowl and rub in the margarine. Blend the yeast, sugar and water together and pour into the flour. Mix to a soft dough and knead for 5 minutes. Cover the bowl with oiled polythene and leave to rise in a warm place for about 1 hour until doubled in size.

Turn the dough on to a floured surface and knead for 5 minutes. Divide the dough into two and shape each piece into a round loaf. Place on a floured baking sheet, or put the dough into two 450-g (1-lb) loaf tins. Cover with oiled polythene; leave in a warm place to prove until the dough doubles in size or rises to the tops of the tins. Bake in the oven at 200°C (400°F) mark 6 for 45 minutes–1 hour until well risen and golden brown. *Makes 2 450-g (1-lb) loaves*
○ *Calories 1593 (6594) per loaf*

Soda bread

450 g (1 lb) wholemeal flour
225 g (8 oz) plain white flour
7·5 ml (1½ level tsp) salt
7·5 ml (1½ level tsp) bicarbonate of soda
50 g (2 oz) Flora
50 g (2 oz) currants
400 ml (¾ pint) skimmed milk
juice of 1 lemon

Stir the flours, salt and bicarbonate of soda together in a mixing bowl. Rub in the margarine and stir in the currants. Mix to a soft dough with the skimmed milk and lemon juice. Turn on to a floured surface and knead gently. Shape into a large round about 5 cm (2 in) thick. Place on a floured baking sheet and cut or score into quarters. Bake in the oven at 200°C (400°F) mark 6

for 40–45 minutes until the bread sounds hollow when tapped on the bottom.
○ *Calories 2831 (11668), whole recipe*

Fluffy bran muffins

225 g (8 oz) self raising flour
100 g (4 oz) bran
50 g (2 oz) wheatgerm
1·25 ml (¼ level tsp) salt
3·75 ml (¾ level tsp) bicarbonate of soda
225 ml (8 fl oz) low fat natural yogurt
150 ml (¼ pint) skimmed milk
50 g (2 oz) black treacle
25 g (1 oz) Flora
50 g (2 oz) seedless raisins

Stir the dry ingredients together in a mixing bowl. Add the yogurt and skimmed milk. Heat the treacle and margarine together in a pan until melted. Cool, then add to the mixture in the bowl with the raisins. Beat together until smooth. Place spoonfuls of the mixture in greased patty tins and bake in the oven at 220°C (425°F) mark 7 for 15–20 minutes until well risen and golden brown. Serve warm. *Makes 18–20*
○ *Calories 1740 (7300), whole recipe*

Chocolate and orange buns

100 g (4 oz) self raising flour
5 ml (1 level tsp) baking powder
100 g (4 oz) Flora
100 g (4 oz) caster sugar
2 eggs, beaten
15 ml (1 level tbsp) cocoa powder
15 ml (1 tbsp) hot water
grated rind of 1 orange
orange food colouring
chocolate buttons to decorate

For the icing
100 g (4 oz) icing sugar, sifted
juice of ½ orange

Sift the flour and baking powder together into a mixing bowl. Add the margarine, sugar and eggs and beat with a wooden spoon for 2–3 minutes until light and fluffy. Divide the mixture in half.

Blend the cocoa to a smooth paste with the hot water. Mix one half of the cake mixture with the blended cocoa, and add the grated orange rind to the other half with some orange food colouring if liked. Place a teaspoon of each mixture in paper cases inside patty tins. Do not mix the orange and chocolate together. Bake in the oven at 190°C (375°F) mark 5 for 12–15 minutes until well risen and golden brown.

Mix the icing sugar with the orange juice and add orange food colouring if liked. Use a teaspoonful to ice each bun and decorate with chocolate buttons. *Makes 12–14*
● *Calories 2603 (10932), whole recipe*

Orange and sultana fruit loaf

200 ml ($\frac{1}{3}$ pint) skimmed milk
2·5 ml ($\frac{1}{2}$ level tsp) bicarbonate of soda
50 g (2 oz) Flora
200 g (7 oz) plain flour
25 g (1 oz) bran
2·5 ml ($\frac{1}{2}$ level tsp) ground cinnamon
100 g (4 oz) soft brown sugar
225 g (8 oz) sultanas
50 g (2 oz) walnuts, chopped
grated rind of 1 orange
30 ml (2 tbsp) orange juice

Blend the milk with the bicarbonate of soda. Place all the ingredients in a mixing

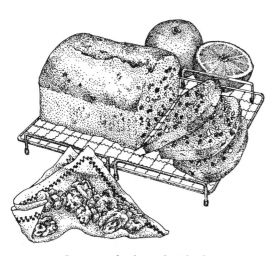

Orange and sultana fruit loaf

bowl and beat together for 5 minutes. Place in a greased and bottom-lined 1·4 litre (2$\frac{1}{2}$ pint) loaf tin. Bake at 160°C (325°F) mark 3 for about 2 hours or until firm to the touch.
○ *Calories 2592 (10550), whole recipe*

Date crunchies

Illustrated in colour facing page 80

175 g (6 oz) rolled oats
75 g (3 oz) Flora
75 g (3 oz) demerara sugar
1·25 ml ($\frac{1}{4}$ level tsp) mixed spice
225 g (8 oz) stoned dates, chopped

Place all the ingredients except the dates in a mixing bowl. Mix together and place half the mixture in an 18-cm (7-in) sandwich tin. Layer the dates on top and cover with the remaining oat mixture. Press down well and bake at 180°C (350°F) mark 4 for 15 minutes. When cool cut into wedges.
○ *Calories 2250 (9190), whole recipe*

Low-cholesterol orange Victoria sandwich

150 g (5 oz) Flora
100 g (4 oz) caster sugar
grated rind of 1 orange
2 egg whites, whisked until stiff
100 g (4 oz) self raising flour, sifted
30 ml (2 level tbsp) orange jelly marmalade
crystallised orange segments to decorate

For the orange icing
75 g (3 oz) icing sugar, sifted
juice of 1 orange

Place the margarine, caster sugar and orange rind in a mixing bowl. Cream with a wooden spoon or electric mixer until light and fluffy. Fold in the whisked egg whites and flour. Place the mixture in two greased and floured 18-cm (7-in) sandwich tins. Bake in the oven at 180°C (350°F) mark 4 for 20 minutes or until firm to the touch and slightly shrinking from the sides of the tins. Turn on to a wire rack to cool.

Sandwich the two halves together with the jelly marmalade. Mix the icing sugar with the orange juice until smooth and spread over the top of cake. Decorate with crystallised orange segments. *Serves 12*
○ *Calories 2624 (10886), whole recipe 218 (907) per slice*

Almond lace wafers

100 g (4 oz) Flora
100 g (4 oz) ground almonds
100 g (4 oz) caster sugar
15 ml (1 level tbsp) plain flour
30 ml (2 tbsp) skimmed milk

Place all the ingredients in a small saucepan and heat gently, stirring, until the fat melts. Drop teaspoonfuls, 10 cm (4 in) apart, on to greased baking sheets. Bake in the oven one sheet at a time at 190°C (375°F) mark 5 until the edges of the biscuits are brown and the centres are bubbling. Allow to stand for 1 minute, then lift each wafer on to a greased rolling pin with a palette knife and leave to harden. Allow to cool on a wire tray. *Makes about 24*
○ *Calories 1992 (9072), whole recipe*

Applenut spice squares

Illustrated in colour facing page 80

For the base
100 g (4 oz) plain flour, sifted
5 ml (1 level tsp) bicarbonate of soda
2·5 ml ($\frac{1}{2}$ level tsp) ground cinnamon
pinch ground cloves
50 g (2 oz) Flora
100 g (4 oz) granulated sugar
$\frac{1}{2}$ beaten egg
50 g (2 oz) walnuts, coarsely chopped
75 g (3 oz) sultanas
150 ml ($\frac{1}{4}$ pint) apple purée

For the topping
50 g (2 oz) walnuts, chopped
50 g (2 oz) demerara sugar

Stir all the base ingredients well together in a large mixing bowl. Turn into a greased

and lined Swiss roll tin. Mix together the topping ingredients and sprinkle over the base. Bake in the oven at 180°C (350°F) mark 4 for about 50 minutes until firm to the touch. Cut into squares and leave to cool. *Makes about 18*
◑ *Calories 2446 (9904), whole recipe*

Prune bread

grated rind and juice 1 orange
175 g (6 oz) stoned prunes, chopped
400 g (14 oz) plain flour
7·5 ml (1$\frac{1}{2}$ level tsp) baking powder
2·5 ml ($\frac{1}{2}$ level tsp) bicarbonate of soda
2·5 ml ($\frac{1}{2}$ level tsp) salt
175 g (6 oz) brown sugar
75 g (3 oz) walnuts, roughly chopped
1 egg, beaten
50 g (2 oz) Flora, melted

Make the orange juice up to 225 ml (8 fl oz) with water. Add the prunes and soak overnight.
Sift the flour, baking powder, bicarbonate of soda and salt into a mixing bowl. Add all the remaining ingredients and mix well for 5 minutes. Place the mixture in a greased and lined 900-g (2-lb) loaf tin and bake in the oven at 180°C (350°F) mark 4 for 1–1$\frac{1}{2}$ hours until well risen and golden.
◑ *Calories 3336 (13726), whole recipe*

Nutty scones

For the scone mixture
50 g (2 oz) Flora
225 g (8 oz) self raising flour, sifted
5 ml (1 level tsp) baking powder
25 g (1 oz) caster sugar
105 ml (7 tbsp) skimmed milk

For the filling
50 g (2 oz) walnuts, chopped
25 g (1 oz) demerara sugar
1·25 ml ($\frac{1}{4}$ level tsp) mixed spice

Place all scone ingredients in a mixing bowl and mix with a wooden spoon to form a soft dough. Knead lightly on a floured surface; roll out to a rectangle 22 × 13 cm (9 × 5 in).

Mix the filling ingredients together and spread over two thirds of the dough. Fold in three and roll out until the dough is 1 cm (½ in) thick. Cut into rounds with a 5-cm (2-in) cutter. Place on a greased baking sheet and brush with milk. Bake in the oven at 220°C (425°F) mark 7 for 10–12 minutes until golden brown. Cool on a wire rack. Serve spread with Flora. *Makes 16*
○ *Calories 102 (399) per scone*

Orange flapjacks

75 g (3 oz) Flora
50 g (2 oz) demerara sugar
30 ml (2 level tbsp) golden syrup
175 g (6 oz) rolled oats
grated rind and juice of 1 orange

Heat the margarine, sugar and syrup together in a saucepan until melted. Pour on to the rolled oats and stir in the grated orange rind and juice. Mix well and spoon the mixture into a greased 20·5-cm (8-in) square cake tin, pressing down well. Bake in the oven at 180°C (350°F) mark 4 for 40–45 minutes. When cool cut into fingers. *Makes 16–20*
○ *Calories 1680 (5880), whole recipe*

Chocolate orange cake

175 g (6 oz) self raising flour, sifted
5 ml (1 level tsp) baking powder
22·5 ml (1½ level tbsp) cocoa powder
30 ml (2 tbsp) hot water
175 g (6 oz) Flora
175 g (6 oz) caster sugar
3 eggs, beaten
icing sugar, sifted, to dredge

For the filling
1 orange, peeled and segmented
30 ml (2 level tbsp) low fat natural yogurt
5 ml (1 tsp) artificial sweetener
100 g (4 oz) curd cheese

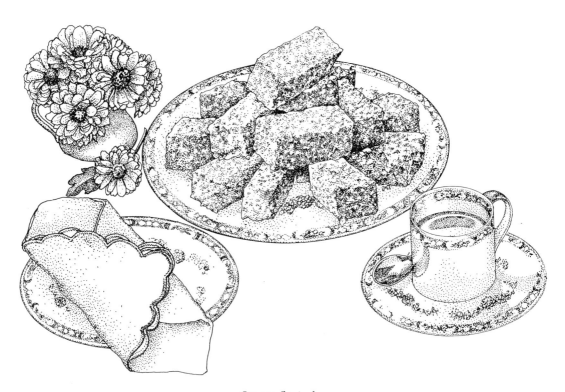

Orange flapjacks

Sift the flour and baking powder together into a mixing bowl. Blend the cocoa and water to a smooth paste and add to the flour. Add the margarine, sugar and eggs to the ingredients in the mixing bowl and beat with a wooden spoon until light and fluffy. Divide the mixture between two greased and lined 18-cm (7-in) sandwich tins. Bake at 170°C (325°F) mark 3 for 25–30 minutes until well risen and golden. Cool.

For the filling, reserve six orange segments for decoration and chop the remainder. Mix the filling ingredients together and spread over one of the sponges. Sandwich the two cakes together, dredge the top of the cake with icing sugar and decorate with the reserved orange segments. *Serves 12*

⬤ *Calories 3305 (13708), whole recipe 275 (1142), per slice*

Nutty buns

For the bun dough
10 g (scant ½ oz) fresh yeast
100 ml (4 fl oz) tepid milk
225 g (8 oz) strong plain flour
5 ml (1 level tsp) salt
25 g (1 oz) Flora
½ egg, beaten

For the topping
25 g (1 oz) Flora
50 g (2 oz) soft brown sugar
50 g (2 oz) nuts, chopped

For the filling
15 g (½ oz) Flora
15 g (½ oz) soft brown sugar
1·25 ml (¼ level tsp) mixed spice
grated rind of 1 orange

For the dough, blend the yeast with the tepid milk and add to 75 g (3 oz) of the flour. Mix together and leave to sponge in a warm place for 15 minutes. Sift the remaining flour and salt into a bowl and rub in the margarine. Add the yeast mixture and egg and mix to a soft dough. Knead for 5

minutes. Cover with oiled polythene and leave in a warm place until doubled in size.

For the topping, melt the margarine in a saucepan and stir in the sugar and nuts. Press into the bottom of an 18-cm (7-in) round cake tin. Knead the dough for 5 minutes on a lightly floured surface. Roll out to an 18-cm (7-in) square. Spread over the margarine for the filling and sprinkle with the sugar, spice and orange rind. Roll up, cut into six and place, cut sides down, in the tin. Cover with oiled polythene and leave in a warm place to prove. Bake in the oven at 230°C (450°F) mark 8 for 10–12 minutes until well risen and golden brown. Turn out and cool on a wire rack. *Makes 6*

◗ *Calories 346 (1336) per bun*

Peanut butter cookies

Illustrated in colour facing page 80

175 g (6 oz) Flora
175 g (6 oz) crunchy peanut butter
225 g (8 oz) light brown sugar
2 eggs, beaten
30 ml (2 tbsp) skimmed milk
350 g (12 oz) plain flour
5 ml (1 level tsp) baking powder
5 ml (1 level tsp) ground ginger
2·5 ml (½ level tsp) ground cloves
pinch salt
225 g (8 oz) salted peanuts, chopped

Cream together the margarine, peanut butter and sugar until light and fluffy. Add the eggs and milk and beat until smooth. Add the sifted dry ingredients and peanuts and stir until thoroughly combined. Place teaspoonfuls of the mixture, 5 cm (2 in) apart, on ungreased baking sheets. Bake in the oven at 190°C (375°F) mark 5 for 10–12 minutes until light brown in colour. Allow to stand for 1 minute before removing from the baking sheets, then leave to cool on a wire rack. *Makes about 50*

◗ *Calories 110 (403) per cookie*

Snacks and Savouries

Chicken lasagne

100 g (4 oz) lasagne verdi
15 g ($\frac{1}{2}$ oz) Flora
1 onion, skinned and chopped
1 clove of garlic, skinned and crushed
425-g (15-oz) can tomatoes
2·5 ml ($\frac{1}{2}$ level tsp) dried oregano
225 g (8 oz) cooked chicken meat, cubed
salt and freshly ground black pepper
150 ml ($\frac{1}{4}$ pint) low fat natural yogurt
paprika to garnish

For the cheese sauce
25 g (1 oz) Flora
25 g (1 oz) flour
400 ml ($\frac{3}{4}$ pint) skimmed milk
75 g (3 oz) Edam cheese, grated

Cook the lasagne in boiling salted water for 12–15 minutes. Drain well. Melt the margarine in a saucepan and cook the onion and garlic for 5 minutes until soft. Add the tomatoes, oregano, chicken and seasoning and cook for 5 minutes. For the cheese sauce, place the margarine, flour and milk in a saucepan. Bring to the boil, stirring continuously until thick and smooth. Add two thirds of the cheese and cook gently until melted.

Place the lasagne, chicken mixture and cheese sauce in alternate layers in an oven-proof dish, finishing with cheese sauce. Sprinkle with the remaining cheese and cook in the oven at 190°C (375°F) mark 5 for 30 minutes until golden brown and bubbling.

Pour the yogurt over the cheese and return to the oven to bake for 5 minutes. Sprinkle with a little paprika and serve immediately.

◗ *Calories 428 (1785)*

Courgettes with tuna

50 g (2 oz) Flora
4 courgettes, cut in half lengthways
99-g (3$\frac{1}{2}$-oz) can tuna, drained and flaked
2 tomatoes, skinned and chopped
1 onion, skinned and grated
1 clove of garlic, skinned and crushed
50 g (2 oz) Edam cheese, grated
15 ml (1 tbsp) chopped parsley

Melt the margarine in a frying pan and cook the courgettes, cut sides down, for 5–10 minutes until softened. Remove from the pan and scoop out the flesh, leaving the skins intact. Chop the flesh and mix with the tuna, tomatoes, onion and garlic. Pile the mixture back into the cases, and sprinkle the tops with the cheese and parsley. Place the courgette halves in an ovenproof dish and cook in the oven at 200°C (400°F) mark 6 for 25–30 minutes until the cheese has melted.

◗ *Calories 236 (916)*

Herby pizza baps

100 g (4 oz) Flora
5–10 ml (1–2 level tsp) dried mixed herbs
5 ml (1 level tsp) paprika
4 wholemeal baps, split
50 g (2 oz) lean cooked ham, sliced
100 g (4 oz) Edam cheese, grated
60-g (2-oz) can anchovy fillets, drained
stuffed olives, halved

Cream together the margarine, herbs and paprika and spread on the halved baps. Place slices of ham on top and sprinkle with the grated Edam. Arrange a lattice of anchovies on top, garnish with the halved olives and cook under a hot grill until the cheese is bubbling and golden. Serve with a salad.

◗ *Calories 484 (2146)*

Braised celery with cheese

15 g (½ oz) Flora
1 onion, skinned and chopped
1 clove of garlic, skinned and crushed
150 ml (¼ pint) dry white wine
150 ml (¼ pint) cider
1 head celery, washed and trimmed
100 g (4 oz) lean cooked ham, chopped
salt and freshly ground pepper
paprika to garnish

For the sauce
25 g (1 oz) Flora
25 g (1 oz) flour
50 g (2 oz) Edam cheese, grated

Melt the margarine in a saucepan and fry the onion and garlic for 5 minutes until soft. Stir in the wine and cider. Lay the sticks of celery in an ovenproof dish, sprinkle the ham on top, and pour over the wine and cider mixture. Season, cover with foil and cook in the oven at 180°C (350°F) mark 4 for 30–35 minutes until tender.

Strain the poaching liquid into a jug. Cover the celery and keep warm.

For the sauce, place the margarine, flour and poaching liquid in a saucepan and bring to boil over a gentle heat, stirring continuously until thickened. Stir in the cheese and pour the sauce over the celery. Sprinkle with paprika; serve with salad.

◗ *Calories 228 (932)*

Leeks in yogurt sauce

juice of 1 lemon
300 ml (½ pint) water
salt
6 peppercorns
3 coriander seeds
6 sprigs parsley
1 onion, skinned and chopped
bay leaf
4 leeks, trimmed
4 slices lean cooked ham
chopped parsley to garnish

For the sauce
300 ml (½ pint) low fat natural yogurt
10 ml (2 tsp) lemon juice
salt and freshly ground black pepper
2·5 ml (½ level tsp) made mustard

Put the lemon juice, water, seasoning, spices, parsley, onion and bay leaf in a saucepan and bring to the boil. Simmer for 10 minutes. Strain. Slit the leeks halfway down their length from the top, open out and wash thoroughly. Put the leeks in a frying pan with the strained liquid. Cover the pan with a lid and simmer gently for 10–15 minutes until soft. Cool in the liquid.

Mix all the sauce ingredients together. Wrap one ham slice around each leek and place lengthways in a serving dish. Pour the sauce over the leeks and garnish with chopped parsley.

◗ *Calories 125 (525)*

Paella

Illustrated in colour facing page 81

50 g (2 oz) Flora
1 onion, skinned and chopped
100 g (4 oz) long grain rice
175-g (6-oz) lean cooked gammon rasher,
    cubed
175 g (6 oz) smoked haddock, cooked and
    flaked
425-g (15-oz) can tomatoes
5 ml (1 level tsp) turmeric
226-g (8-oz) packet frozen sweetcorn, peas
    and peppers
salt and freshly ground black pepper
chopped parsley to garnish

Melt the margarine in a large frying pan
and fry the onion for 5 minutes until softened. Add the rice and fry for 2 minutes.
Stir in the gammon, haddock, tomatoes
and turmeric and simmer gently for 20
minutes. If necessary add a little water
during cooking to keep the mixture moist.
Stir in the vegetables and seasoning, bring
back to the boil and simmer gently for a
further 3–4 minutes. Sprinkle the paella
with the freshly chopped parsley just before
serving.
◑ *Calories 402 (1714)*

Spicy meat pasties

225 g (8 oz) all-in-one shortcrust pastry (see
    page 100)
15 g (½ oz) Flora
1 onion, skinned and chopped
175 g (6 oz) cooked chicken or lamb, diced
15 ml (1 level tbsp) tomato ketchup
2·5 ml (½ tsp) Worcestershire sauce
salt and freshly ground black pepper
50 g (2 oz) Edam cheese, grated
60 ml (4 tbsp) skimmed milk

Roll out the pastry dough and cut twelve
10-cm (4-in) circles with a round cutter.
Melt the margarine in a saucepan and fry
the onion for 5 minutes until soft. Add the
meat, tomato ketchup, Worcestershire
sauce, seasoning and grated cheese. Spoon

the mixture on to half of the circles and
moisten the edges with water. Top with the
remaining pastry circles, seal and flute the
edges. Brush with the milk and bake in the
oven at 200°C (400°F) mark 6 for 20–25
minutes. *Makes 6*
◑ *Calories 416 (1684)*

Baked potato with creamed celery

4 even-sized potatoes, scrubbed
50 g (2 oz) Flora
1 onion, skinned and chopped
2 sticks of celery, washed and finely chopped
50 g (2 oz) cottage cheese
30 ml (2 tbsp) chopped parsley
salt and freshly ground black pepper

Grease the skins of the potatoes with 25 g
(1 oz) of the margarine. Place on a baking
sheet and bake in the oven at 180°C
(350°F) mark 4 for 1½–2 hours until soft
when pinched.
    Melt the remaining margarine in a sauce-
pan and fry the onion and celery with the
cottage cheese and parsley. Alternatively
mix the ingredients together and rub
through a sieve. Season well. Split the
potatoes nearly in half, fill with celery mixture and return to the oven for a further
5–10 minutes.
○ *Calories 250 (1021)*

Stuffed peppers with smoked haddock

4 green peppers
100 g (4 oz) smoked haddock
200 ml (⅓ pint) water
25 g (1 oz) Flora
1 onion, skinned and finely chopped
50 g (2 oz) long grain rice
15 ml (1 level tbsp) tomato paste
6 gherkins, sliced
juice of 1 lemon

Cut the tops off the peppers and remove the

seeds. Poach the fish in the water with half the margarine for 5 minutes until tender. Remove the fish and flake it. Reserve the poaching liquid. Melt the remaining margarine in a saucepan and fry the onion for 5 minutes until softened. Stir in the rice and cook for another 2 minutes. Add the reserved poaching liquid and simmer gently for 10–15 minutes until the rice is tender.

Stir the haddock, tomato paste, gherkins and lemon juice into the rice and divide the mixture between the peppers. Place in an ovenproof dish, cover with foil and cook in the oven at 200°C (400°F) mark 6 for 20–25 minutes until the peppers are tender.

◗ *Calories 175 (693)*

Chicken stuffed cabbage leaves

1 medium cabbage

For the filling
25 g (1 oz) Flora
1 onion, skinned and sliced
350 g (12 oz) cooked chicken meat, chopped
50 g (2 oz) cooked long grain rice
30 ml (2 level tbsp) tomato paste
salt and freshly ground black pepper

For the tomato sauce
25 g (1 oz) Flora
1 onion, skinned and chopped
15 ml (1 level tbsp) flour
425-g (15-oz) can tomatoes
salt and freshly ground black pepper
1·25 ml ($\frac{1}{4}$ level tsp) dried mixed herbs

Chicken stuffed cabbage leaves

Separate the cabbage leaves, wash and blanch in boiling salted water for 3 minutes. Drain on kitchen paper towel. Melt the margarine in a saucepan and gently fry the onion for 5 minutes. Add the remaining filling ingredients and mix well. Place a spoonful of filling on each cabbage leaf and roll up like a parcel, tucking the ends underneath. Arrange in an ovenproof dish.

For the sauce, melt the margarine in a saucepan and fry the onion for 5 minutes. Stir in the flour and add the tomatoes, seasoning and herbs. Pour the sauce over the stuffed cabbage leaves and cook in the oven at 190°C (375°F) mark 5 for 25–30 minutes.

◖ *Calories 321 (1306)*

Veal meatballs in tomato sauce

450 g (1 lb) lean minced veal
15 ml (1 tbsp) skimmed milk
15 ml (1 tbsp) chopped parsley
2·5 ml ($\frac{1}{2}$ level tsp) dried thyme
salt and freshly ground pepper
1·25 ml ($\frac{1}{4}$ level tsp) grated nutmeg
50 g (2 oz) fresh white breadcrumbs
1 egg, beaten
30 ml (2 level tbsp) seasoned flour
sunflower oil for frying

For the sauce
25 g (1 oz) Flora
15 ml (1 level tbsp) plain flour
300 ml ($\frac{1}{2}$ pint) beef stock
226-g (8-oz) can tomatoes
bay leaf
salt and freshly ground black pepper

In a large bowl mix together the veal, milk, herbs, seasoning, nutmeg, breadcrumbs and egg. Shape into 10–12 meatballs and roll in the seasoned flour. Fry in sunflower oil for 10–15 minutes until golden brown. Drain on kitchen paper towel and place in an ovenproof dish.

For the sauce, melt the margarine in a saucepan, stir in the flour and cook for 2 minutes. Gradually stir in the beef stock, bring to the boil and cook for 2 minutes,

stirring. Add the tomatoes with their juice and the bay leaf. Season to taste and simmer for 5 minutes. Remove the bay leaf and purée the sauce in a blender or rub through a sieve. Pour over the meatballs, cover the dish with a lid or foil and cook in the oven at 180°C (350°F) mark 4 for 15–20 minutes.

◖ *Calories 381 (1420)*

Piquant chicken

450 g (1 lb) cooked chicken meat, chopped
salt and freshly ground black pepper
150 ml ($\frac{1}{4}$ pint) low fat natural yogurt
175 g (6 oz) long grain rice
100 g (4 oz) frozen peas
99-g ($3\frac{1}{2}$-oz) can pimientos, drained and sliced

For the sauce
25 g (1 oz) Flora
25 g (1 oz) flour
300 ml ($\frac{1}{2}$ pint) chicken stock
30 ml (2 tbsp) lemon juice
5 ml (1 level tsp) chilli powder

For the sauce, place all the ingredients in a saucepan, bring to the boil over a moderate heat, stirring continuously, and cook for 2–3 minutes until thickened and smooth. Add the chicken, seasoning and yogurt and cook gently over a low heat. Do not boil.

Meanwhile, cook the rice in boiling sal-

Veal meatballs in tomato sauce

ted water for 10–15 minutes until tender. Drain, add the peas and pimientos and cook over a low heat for 5–10 minutes. Arrange the rice round the edge of a heated serving dish and spoon the chicken mixture into the centre.

◑ *Calories 442 (1861)*

Brown rice pilaf

100 g (4 oz) brown rice
300 ml (½ pint) boiling water
½ chicken stock cube, crumbled
50 g (2 oz) mushrooms, sliced
2·5 ml (½ level tsp) salt
freshly ground black pepper
1·25 ml (¼ level tsp) dried thyme
2 sticks of celery, washed and thinly sliced
1 green pepper, seeded and chopped
100 g (4 oz) cooked chicken meat, chopped

Place the first seven ingredients in an oven-proof dish. Cover and cook in the oven at 180°C (350°F) mark 4 for 1 hour. Stir in the celery, pepper and chicken. Replace the lid and return to the oven to cook for a further 15 minutes. Fluff up the rice with a fork before serving.

◑ *Calories 152 (693)*

Kipper kedgeree

175 g (6 oz) long grain rice
450 g (1 lb) kippers, poached
1 egg, hard-boiled and chopped
141-g (5-oz) packet frozen peas, cooked
50 g (2 oz) Flora
chopped parsley to garnish

Grease a 1·2-litre (2-pint) casserole dish. Cook the rice in boiling salted water for 10–12 minutes. Rinse under hot water and drain. Flake the fish, removing all skin and bones, and add to the rice with the egg and peas. Mix together and place in the prepared dish. Dot with knobs of margarine and cook in the oven at 170°C (325°F) mark 3 for 15–20 minutes. Sprinkle with chopped parsley and serve immediately.

◑ *Calories 562 (2188)*

Garlic bread

Illustrated in colour facing page 81

1 French loaf
2 cloves of garlic, skinned
1·25 ml (¼ level tsp) salt
50 g (2 oz) Flora

Slice through the French loaf almost to the base at 2·5-cm (1-in) intervals. Crush the garlic with the salt and beat into the margarine. Spread this mixture on both sides of each cut in the loaf. Press together to reshape the loaf and wrap in foil. Bake in the oven at 200°C (400°F) mark 6 for 20 minutes. Serve with soup, pâté or cheese.

◯ *Calories 260 (1054)*

Wholemeal pizza

For the pizza base
100 g (4 oz) plain white flour, sifted
100 g (4 oz) wholemeal flour
2·5 ml (½ level tsp) salt
15 g (½ oz) Flora
15 g (½ oz) fresh yeast
15 g (½ oz) caster sugar
200 ml (⅓ pint) tepid water
sunflower oil

For the topping
15 g (½ oz) Flora
1 onion, skinned and chopped
425-g (15-oz) can tomatoes
2·5 ml (½ level tsp) dried oregano
2·5 ml (½ level tsp) dried thyme
salt and freshly ground black pepper
100 g (4 oz) Edam cheese, thinly sliced
1 green or red pepper, seeded and sliced

For the pizza base, mix the flours and salt together in a warm bowl and rub in the margarine. Blend the yeast, sugar and water together and add to the flour. Mix to a soft dough and knead for 5 minutes. Cover the dough with oiled polythene and leave in a warm place to rise until doubled in size.

Turn the dough on to a floured surface and knead for 5 minutes. Roll out into a long strip, brush with oil and roll up like a

Swiss roll. Repeat this twice, then roll out the dough to a 23-cm (9-in) round. Place on an oiled baking sheet.

For the topping, melt the margarine in a saucepan and fry the onion for 5 minutes until soft. Add the remaining ingredients except the Edam and sliced pepper; heat through for 5 minutes. Spread the mixture over the pizza base, arrange the slices of Edam and pepper over the top and bake in the oven at 230°C (450°F) mark 8 for 20–30 minutes.

○ *Calories 389 (1781)*

Tunafish tartlets

For the herby pastry
225 g (8 oz) plain flour
pinch salt
15 ml (1 level tbsp) dried mixed herbs
125 g (4 oz) Flora

For the filling
25 g (1 oz) Flora
1 onion, skinned and finely chopped
25 g (1 oz) flour
300 ml (½ pint) skimmed milk
210-g (7½-oz) can tuna, drained and flaked
salt and freshly ground black pepper
75 g (3 oz) Edam cheese, grated

For the pastry, sift the flour, salt and herbs together and rub in the margarine until the mixture resembles fine breadcrumbs. Add enough cold water to mix to a smooth dough. Knead gently and turn on to a lightly floured surface. Roll out and use to line 10–12 patty tins. Chill.

For the filling, melt the margarine in a saucepan and fry the onion for 10 minutes until light brown. Stir in the flour and cook for 1 minute. Gradually stir in the milk. Bring to the boil, stirring, and cook for 2 minutes until the sauce thickens. Stir in the tuna fish and seasoning. Divide the sauce between the pastry cases and sprinkle with grated cheese. Bake in the oven at 200°C (400°F) mark 6 for 30 minutes until golden brown. *Makes 10–12*

◑ *Calories   288 (1214) per tartlet (10)*
241 (1012) per tartlet (12)

Spaghetti with tuna sauce

25 g (1 oz) Flora
1 large onion, skinned and chopped
1 clove of garlic, skinned and crushed
2 210-g (7½-oz) cans tuna, well drained and flaked
425-g (15-oz) can tomatoes
15 ml (1 level tbsp) tomato paste
5 ml (1 level tsp) dried oregano
175 g (6 oz) spaghetti
50 g (2 oz) Edam cheese, finely grated

Melt the margarine in a large saucepan and gently fry the onion and garlic for 10 minutes until golden. Stir in the tuna, tomatoes, tomato paste and oregano. Simmer gently for 15–20 minutes.

Meanwhile, cook the spaghetti in boiling salted water for 10–15 minutes. Drain and serve with the sauce and a separate small bowl of the grated cheese.

◑ *Calories 518 (2180)*

Sauces and Dressings

French dressing

150 ml (¼ pint) sunflower oil
75 ml (5 tbsp) wine vinegar or lemon juice
1·25 ml (¼ level tsp) pepper
2·5 ml (½ level tsp) salt
1·25 ml (¼ level tsp) sugar
1·25 ml (¼ level tsp) made mustard
15 ml (1 tbsp) chopped fresh chives, optional

Place all the ingredients in a screw-topped jar and shake well. Store in the refrigerator and use as required.
○ *Calories 1280 (5287), whole recipe*

Sunflower mayonnaise

1·25 ml (¼ level tsp) sugar
2·5 ml (½ level tsp) dry mustard
1·25 ml (¼ level tsp) salt
pinch cayenne pepper
20 ml (4 tsp) white wine vinegar or lemon juice
1 egg white
200 ml (⅓ pint) sunflower oil

Put the sugar and seasonings in a small bowl and blend with 5 ml (1 tsp) of the vinegar or lemon juice. Whisk the egg white until thick but not stiff, using a rotary beater. Add half the oil, a little at a time, beating well after each addition. Continue beating while adding the blended seasonings and vinegar. Add the remaining oil gradually and then the remaining vinegar or lemon juice. Chill and use as required.
○ *Calories 1735 (7607), whole recipe*

Herby tomato sauce

15 g (½ oz) Flora
1 large onion, skinned and chopped
1 clove of garlic, skinned and crushed
45 ml (3 level tbsp) tomato paste
450 g (1 lb) tomatoes, skinned and chopped
5 ml (1 level tsp) dried oregano
300 ml (½ pint) beef stock
7·5 ml (1½ level tsp) caster sugar
salt and freshly ground black pepper
1 bay leaf

Melt the margarine in a saucepan, add the onion and garlic and fry gently for 10 minutes until soft. Add the remaining ingredients, stir well, cover and simmer gently for about 30 minutes. Remove the bay leaf and purée in a blender or rub through a sieve. Reheat gently and serve.
○ *Calories 79 (313), whole recipe*

Quick hollandaise sauce

30 ml (2 tbsp) hot water
120 ml (8 level tbsp) sunflower mayonnaise
  (see recipe on page 113)
5 ml (1 tsp) lemon juice
salt and freshly ground white pepper

Blend the hot water into the mayonnaise. Stir in a heatproof bowl standing in a pan of hot water until blended and heated through. Stir in the lemon juice and seasoning and mix well.
○ *Calories 1085 (4054), whole recipe*

Lemon chive dressing

100 g (4 oz) cottage cheese
10 ml (2 tsp) lemon juice
30 ml (2 tbsp) French dressing (see page 113)
salt and freshly ground pepper
15 ml (1 tbsp) chopped fresh chives

Sieve the cottage cheese into a bowl and stir in the other ingredients. Alternatively, use a blender to mix all the ingredients until smooth. Chill the dressing thoroughly before serving.
○ *Calories 285 (1149), whole recipe*

Creamy chive dressing

141-g (5-oz) carton low fat natural yogurt
15 ml (1 tbsp) chopped fresh chives
5 ml (1 tsp) lemon juice
1·25 ml (¼ level tsp) dry mustard
salt and freshly ground black pepper

Mix all the ingredients well together. Add 1·25 ml (¼ level tsp) garlic salt or 2·5 ml (½ level tsp) curry powder to vary the flavour.
○ *Calories 55 (229), whole recipe*

All-in-one sauce

POURING SAUCE

15 g (½ oz) Flora
15 g (½ oz) flour
300 ml (½ pint) skimmed or filled milk (see page 116)
salt and freshly ground white pepper

Place all the ingredients in a saucepan. Bring to the boil over a moderate heat, stirring continuously, and cook for 2–3 minutes until thickened and smooth.
○ *Calories 380 (1504), whole recipe (using filled milk)*

COATING SAUCE

25 g (1 oz) Flora
25 g (1 oz) flour
300 ml (½ pint) skimmed or filled milk (see page 116)
salt and freshly ground white pepper

Follow the instructions for All-in-one pouring sauce (see above)
○ *Calories 535 (2090), whole recipe (using filled milk)*

Variations

The basic white sauces can be varied as follows:

CAPER SAUCE

Add 15 ml (1 level tbsp) capers and 5 ml (1 tsp) caper vinegar.

Serve with fish.
○ *Calories 380 (1504) pouring sauce, 535 (2090) coating sauce, whole recipe*

CHEESE SAUCE

Add 50–100 g (2–4 oz) grated Edam cheese and 2·5 ml (½ level tsp) made mustard.

Serve with vegetables or fish.
◑ *Calories 555–710 (2236–2821) pouring sauce, 675–850 (710–885) coating sauce, whole recipe*

MUSTARD SAUCE

Add 10 ml (2 level tsp) made mustard and 10 ml (2 tsp) vinegar.

Serve with fish.
○ *Calories 380 (1504) pouring sauce, 535 (2090) coating sauce, whole recipe*

ONION SAUCE

Add 2 large onions, skinned, chopped and boiled.

Serve with lamb.
○ *Calories 435 (8181) pouring sauce, 590 (2319) coating sauce, whole recipe*

PARSLEY SAUCE

Add 15 ml (1 tbsp) chopped parsley.

Serve with white fish.
○ *Calories 380 (1504) pouring sauce, 535 (2090) coating sauce, whole recipe*

Gravy

15 ml (1 tbsp) sunflower oil
15 ml (1 level tbsp) flour
300 ml (½ pint) hot vegetable water or well-flavoured stock
salt and pepper

Heat the oil in a small saucepan, add the flour and blend well. Cook gently until brown, stirring continuously. Gradually add the stock, bring to the boil and cook for 2–3 minutes. Season well, strain and serve hot. If the gravy is very pale, extra colouring can be added by using gravy browning.
○ *Calories 195 (815), whole recipe*

Bread sauce

a few cloves
1 onion, skinned
400 ml (¾ pint) filled milk
75 g (3 oz) fresh breadcrumbs
15 g (½ oz) Flora
salt and pepper

Stick the cloves into the onion, put in a saucepan with the milk and bring almost to the boil. Remove from the heat and allow to stand for 20 minutes. Remove the onion, add the breadcrumbs and margarine and season to taste. Reheat before serving.
○ *Calories 685 (2696), whole recipe*

Barbecue sauce

226-g (8-oz) can tomatoes
2 medium onions, skinned and sliced
15 ml (1 tbsp) dry cider
2·5 ml (½ level tsp) dried basil
salt and pepper
1 clove of garlic, skinned and crushed

Simmer all the ingredients together until well reduced, thick and pulpy. Sieve or blend and adjust the seasoning. This spicy tomato sauce can be served with lean grilled chops, steaks or hamburgers.
○ *Calories 105 (438), whole recipe*

Tartare sauce

150 ml (¼ pint) Sunflower mayonnaise (see page 113)
5 ml (1 tsp) chopped fresh tarragon or chives
10 ml (2 level tsp) chopped capers
10 ml (2 level tsp) chopped gherkins
10 ml (2 tsp) chopped parsley
15 ml (1 tbsp) lemon juice or tarragon vinegar

Mix all the ingredients together well, then leave the sauce to stand for at least 1 hour before serving to allow the flavours to blend. Serve with any simply cooked fish.
○ *Calories 965 (4681), whole recipe*

Dairy Food Substitutes

Polyunsaturated filled milk

On a cholesterol lowering diet, this is the most palatable alternative to whole milk. If you are also on a low calorie diet, use only 15 ml (1 tbsp) sunflower oil or substitute ordinary skimmed milk.

75 ml (5 rounded tbsp) skimmed milk powder
600 ml (1 pint) water
30 ml (2 tbsp) sunflower oil

Blend together the skimmed milk powder and water until smooth. Leave in the refrigerator for 1–2 hours.

Place in a liquidiser with the oil and liquidise for about 2 minutes until thoroughly mixed.

Use and store as ordinary milk.
○ *Calories   440 (1848), whole recipe*
305 (1281), with only 15 ml (1 tbsp) sunflower oil
177 (756), per 568 ml (1 pint) skimmed milk

Home-made low fat yogurt

600 ml (1 pint) skimmed milk
141-g (5-oz) carton natural low fat yogurt

Bring the skimmed milk to the boil, cover and allow to cool to a temperature of 43°C (110°F). Add the yogurt and mix well. Pour the milk into a warmed wide-necked vacuum flask. Seal the flask and leave undisturbed for 8–10 hours to set. Remove the yogurt from the flask by shaking it. Place in a sterilized container and keep in the refrigerator until required. It is important to make sure that the carton of yogurt is absolutely fresh and that a new carton of yogurt is purchased and used for each new supply of home-made yogurt.
○ *Calories 495 (2079), whole recipe*

Home-made cottage cheese

75 g (3 oz) skimmed milk powder
600 ml (1 pint) water
7·5 ml (1½ tsp) rennet

Place the milk powder in a saucepan. Gradually add the water, stirring until dissolved. Heat until just tepid, add the rennet and mix well. Pour into a basin and leave in a warm place until the curd has formed.

Place the basin over a pan of hot water and heat until the curd and whey separate.

Line a strainer with a piece of sterilized muslin and pour in the curd and whey. Tie the ends of the muslin to form a bag, hang and allow to drip for 24 hours.

Place the curd in a basin and mash with a fork. Flavour by adding salt, pepper and chopped chives if you wish.
Calories 270 (1050), whole recipe

Useful Tables

Relative saturated fat and cholesterol content of some commonly used foods

	Saturated fat	Cholesterol		Saturated fat	Cholesterol
CEREALS AND CEREAL PRODUCTS			**Fats** (*contd.*)		
			Oil, vegetable, corn oil	low	nil
Biscuits, plain	medium	low	groundnut	medium	nil
water	low	nil	olive	medium	nil
Bread, brown and white	low	nil	soya bean	low	nil
Cereals, eg cornflakes	low	nil	sunflower	low	nil
Cornflour, custard powder	low	nil			
Flour, white, plain or self			**FISH**		
raising	low	nil	Anchovy	low	high
Macaroni	low	nil	Fish roe and caviare	medium	high
wholewheat	low	nil	Herring and kipper	low	medium
Noodles, plain	low	nil	Mackerel	low	medium
containing egg	medium	medium	Pilchard	low	medium
Oatmeal	low	nil	Prawns and shrimps	low	high
Rice	low	nil	Salmon, canned in oil	low	medium
brown	low	nil	Trout	low	medium
Spaghetti	low	nil	Tuna, canned in oil	low	medium
wholewheat	low	nil	White fish – cod, coley,		
Wheatgerm	low	nil	haddock, hake, halibut,		
			plaice, sole, whiting	low	medium
DRINKS: ALCOHOLIC					
Advocaat	medium	high	**FRUIT**		
Beer	nil	nil	All kinds	nil	nil
Liqueurs	nil	nil			
Spirits	nil	nil	**MEAT AND POULTRY**		
Vermouths	nil	nil	Bacon	high	medium
Wines and fortified wines	nil	nil	Beef, corned	high	medium
			roast	high	medium
DRINKS: NON ALCOHOLIC			trimmed lean	medium	medium
Coffee and tea, black	nil	nil	Brains	high	high
Soft drinks	nil	nil	Chicken	low	medium
			Duck	high	medium
EGGS			Goose	high	medium
Egg, fresh	low	high	Ham, lean	medium	medium
white	nil	nil	Heart	medium	high
yolk	low	high	Kidney	low	high
			Lamb	high	medium
FATS			Liver	low	high
Butter	medium	high	Pork	high	medium
Lard, suet	high	medium	Rabbit	low	medium
Margarine			Sausage, pork	high	medium
Flora	low	nil	Sweetbreads	medium	high
hard	high	nil to medium	Tongue	high	medium
			Turkey	low	medium
soft	medium	nil to medium	Veal	medium	medium
			Venison	low	medium

Relative saturated fat and cholesterol content of some commonly used foods (*contd.*)

	Saturated fat	Cholesterol
MILK AND MILK PRODUCTS		
Buttermilk	low	low
Cheese, full fat – eg Cheddar	high	medium
medium fat – eg Edam	medium	medium
cottage	low	low
curd	medium	low
Cream	high	medium
Milk, evaporated	high	medium
skimmed	low	low
whole	high	medium
Yogurt, natural low fat	low	low
NUTS		
Almonds	low	nil
Coconut	high	nil
Peanuts	medium	nil
Walnuts	low	nil
PRESERVES AND COOKING INGREDIENTS		
Chocolate, milk	medium	medium
Chutney, average	nil	nil
Cocoa powder	medium	nil
Gelatine	nil	nil
Honey	nil	nil
Ice cream, ready made	high	medium
Jam, marmalade	nil	nil
Mayonnaise, ready made	medium	medium
Peanut butter	medium	nil
Sugar	nil	nil

	Saturated fat	Cholesterol
Preserves and cooking ingredients (*contd.*)		
Syrup	nil	nil
Tomato ketchup and purée	nil	nil
VEGETABLES		
Asparagus	nil	nil
Avocado pear	low	nil
Beans, all kinds	nil	nil
Beetroot	nil	nil
Brussels sprouts	nil	nil
Cabbage	nil	nil
Cauliflower	nil	nil
Courgettes	nil	nil
Cucumber	nil	nil
Leeks	nil	nil
Lettuce	nil	nil
Mushrooms, raw	nil	nil
Olives	low	nil
Parsnips	nil	nil
Peas	nil	nil
Peppers, green and red	nil	nil
Potatoes	nil	nil
chips fried in lard	high	nil to medium
crisps	medium to high	nil to medium
Spinach	nil	nil
Swedes	nil	nil
Sweetcorn	nil	nil
Tomatoes	nil	nil
Turnips	nil	nil

Calorie content of some commonly used foods

	Kilojoules kj per 100 g	Kilocalories kcal per oz		Kilojoules per 100 ml	Kilocalories per fl oz
CEREALS AND CEREAL PRODUCTS			Drinks: alcoholic* (contd.)		
All-Bran	1295	88	Liqueurs	1107	75
Arrowroot	1488	101	Rum	919	65
Barley, pearl, dry	1504	102	Sherry, dry	481	33
Biscuits,			sweet	568	38
chocolate	2077	142	Vermouth, dry	585	35
plain	1801	122	Vodka	919	65
rich, sweet	2073	141	Whisky	919	65
Bran	827	51	Wine	271	18
Bread, brown	990	66			
rye	902	54	**DRINKS: NON-ALCOHOLIC***		
malt	1054	62			
starch reduced	978	66	Cordial,		
white	1057	72	undiluted	438	30
wholemeal	1007	68	Grapefruit	250	17
fried	2064	140	Lemon juice	171	12
Buckwheat	1407	83	Orange juice	238	16
Cornflakes	1525	103	Pineapple juice	204	14
Cornflour,			Tomato juice	75	5
custard powder	1475	100	Tonic water	146	10
Crispbread	1329	90			
Flour, white,			**EGGS**		
plain, or self			Eggs, fresh		
raising	1454	99	(Quick measure		
Flour, wholemeal	1351	79	1 large egg =		
Flour, rye	1428	83	90 kcal (376 kj)		
Macaroni, raw	1525	103	1 standard egg =		
Macaroni,			80 kcal (334 kj)	660	45
wholewheat, raw	1525	103	Egg white		
Muesli	1475	100	(Quick measure		
Oatmeal, raw	1672	113	1 egg white =		
Rice, raw	1504	102	15 kcal (62 kj)	158	11
boiled	518	35	Egg yolk		
brown, boiled	518	35	(Quick measure		
Sago, raw	1488	101	1 egg yolk =		
Semolina, raw	1554	109	65 kcal (271 kj)	1454	99
Shredded wheat	1375	93			
Spaghetti, raw	1525	103	**FATS**		
wholewheat, raw	1525	103	Butter	3114	211
Sugar Smacks	1542	105	Lard or compound		
Tapioca	1504	102	white fat	3736	253
Weetabix	1475	100	Margarines	3214	218
Wheatgerm	1475	100	Vegetable oil	3757	255
DRINKS: ALCOHOLIC*			**FISH**		
Beer and stout	132	10	Anchovy		
Brandy	919	65	(Quick measure		
Cider, dry	132	10	1 fillet =		
Gin	919	65	7 kcal (29 kj)	438	30

*The figures in the two columns are for kj per 100 ml and kcal per fl oz

Calorie content of some commonly used foods (*contd.*)

	Kilojoules kj per 100 g	Kilocalories kcal per oz		Kilojoules kj per 100 g	Kilocalories kcal per oz
Fish (*contd.*)			**Fruit** (*contd.*)		
Fish fingers, raw	794	54	Orange juice,		
Herring, raw	794	54	canned,		
Kipper, raw	919	62	unconcentrated	192	13
Mackerel, on bone			Peaches, fresh	158	11
raw	438	30	Pears	171	12
Pilchards, canned			Pineapple, fresh	192	13
in tomato sauce	635	43	Plums, fresh	133	9
Prawns, shelled	438	30	Prunes, dried	672	46
Salmon, canned	555	38	Raisins, dried	1036	70
Sardines,			Raspberries	104	7
canned in oil	1191	81	Rhubarb	29	2
Trout, on bone,			Strawberries	104	7
raw	438	30	Sultanas, dried	1045	71
Tuna, canned					
in oil	1107	75	**MILK AND**		
Whitebait, fried	2244	152	**MILK PRODUCTS**		
White fish, raw			Cheese, Cheddar	1722	117
filleted – cod,			cottage	480	31
haddock, hake,			curd	589	40
halibut, plaice,			Edam	1149	88
sole, coley,			Cream, double –		
whiting	296–367	20–25	30 ml (2 tbsp)	434	104
			single – 30 ml		
			(2 tbsp)	167	40
FRUIT			soured – 30 ml		
Apples, eating or			(2 tbsp)	217	52
cooking	192	13	Milk, dried		
Apricots, dried	760	52	skimmed	1375	93
Apricots, raw	117	8	Milk, liquid		
Bananas	326	22	whole 30 ml		
Blackberries	117	8	(2 tbsp)	75	18
Blackcurrants	117	8	Milk, skimmed		
Canned fruit, in			30 ml (2 tbsp)	37	9
syrup, average	367	25	Buttermilk	159	10
Cherries	192	13	Yogurt, fat free	171	12
glacé	20	137	fruit	326	22
Cranberries	62	4	natural	238	16
Currants, dried	1015	69			
Dates, dried	1036	70	**MEAT AND POULTRY**		
Figs, dried	890	60	Bacon, raw	1989	135
Gooseberries	117	8	Bacon, well		
Grapefruit	91	6	grilled	890	60
Grapes, black			Beef, corned	936	64
or white	221	15	lean mince or		
Lemons	29	2	stewing	890	60
Melon, yellow			silverside,		
with skin	940	4	boiled	1120	83
honeydew			steak for grilling	735	50
with skin	171	12	topside or sirloin		
Oranges	146	10	roasted	1178	80

Calorie content of some commonly used foods (*contd.*)

	Kilojoules kj per 100 g	Kilocalories kcal per oz		Kilojoules kj per 100 g	Kilocalories kcal per oz
Meat and poultry (*contd.*)			**Preserves and cooking ingredients** (*contd.*)		
Chicken, on bone,			Cocoa powder	1876	128
raw	601	30	Cranberry sauce	635	43
flesh only, raw	769	41	Curry powder	986	67
roast meat only	760	52	Gelatine	1036	70
Duck, roast meat			Honey	1208	82
only	1312	89	Jam and		
Frankfurters,			marmalade	1095	74
cooked	1329	90	Mustard, made		trace
Gammon steak,			Malt, dried	1545	92
grilled	589	40	Peanut butter	2508	170
Garlic sausage	1187	71	Sugar	1651	112
Ham, lean boiled	890	60	Syrup, golden	1237	84
Heart, ox raw	438	30	Toffees	1713	120
Kidney, raw	438	30	Tomato ketchup	413	28
Lamb, flesh only,			purée	158	11
average, raw	1387	94	Treacle, black	1078	73
leg, roast meat					
only	1178	80	**VEGETABLES**		
shoulder, roast			Artichokes, globe,		
meat only	1400	95	boiled	58	4
Liver, raw	581	39	Artichokes,		
Luncheon meat	1358	92	Jerusalem,		
Pork chop, on			boiled	75	5
bone, grilled	589	40	Aubergine, raw	58	4
fillet	1036	70	Avocado pear	367	25
leg, roast meat			Beans, baked in		
only	1329	90	tomato sauce	384	26
Rabbit, on bone,			broad	208	19
raw	543	37	green	58	4
Sausage, pork	1542	105	haricot, dried	1078	73
Tongue	1295	88	boiled	367	25
Turkey, roast			butter, raw	1111	76
meat only	819	56	cooked	388	26
Veal, pie, raw	518	35	soya	495	29
roast meat only	973	66	beansprouts	100	6
			Beetroot, boiled	171	12
NUTS			Broccoli, boiled	58	4
Almonds	2424	164	Brussels sprouts,		
Coconut,			raw	133	9
desiccated	2541	172	Cabbage, boiled	29	2
Peanuts, roasted	2449	166	raw	117	8
Walnuts	2227	151	Carrots	104	7
			Cauliflower	104	7
PRESERVES AND			Celery	29	2
COOKING INGREDIENTS			Chicory	45	3
Bovril	338	23	Courgettes	45	3
Capers	75	5	Cucumber	45	3
Chocolate,			Gherkins, pickled	45	3
milk or plain	2441	165	Leeks	113	9
Chutney, average	635	43			

Calorie content of some commonly used foods (*contd.*)

	Kilojoules kj per 100 g	Kilocalories kcal per oz		Kilojoules kj per 100 g	Kilocalories kcal per oz
Vegetables (*contd.*)			Potatoes, boiled	338	23
Lentils, dried	1237	84	fried chips	986	67
Lettuce	45	3	raw	326	22
Marrow	29	2	roast	518	35
Mushrooms	29	2	Pumpkin	58	4
Mustard and cress	45	3	Radishes	58	4
Olives, stuffed	355	24	Seakale	29	2
Onions	104	7	Spinach	91	6
Parsley	204	14	Spring greens	45	3
Parsnips	267	18	Swedes	75	5
Peas, fresh or			Sweetcorn, fresh,		
frozen	267	18	frozen or		
boiled	204	14	canned	397	27
canned			Tomatoes, raw		
processed	297	27	or canned	58	4
Peppers, green			Turnips	75	5
and red	91	6	Watercress	58	4

Fibre content of foods

High
Malt extract
Breads:
Wholewheat
Granary
Rye
Whole wheat
Buck wheat flour
Brown rice
Cereals:
Porridge
Muesli
All-bran
Bran
Nuts
Vegetables (lightly cooked and including any seeds, skins and strings):
Beans
Cabbage
Carrots
Peas
Corn on the cob
Marrow
Potatoes baked in jackets
Turnips
Fruit (raw, with skins):
Apples
Apricots
Berries
Pears
Dried fruits

Medium
Molasses
Honey
Vegetables (cooked without skins, seeds, strings):
Potatoes
Carrots
Beans
Fruit (peeled and cooked):
Apples, Pears, etc.

Low
Bacon
Beef
White bread
Butter
Cheese
Chicken
Cream
Alcoholic drinks
Soft drinks
Eggs
Fish
Ice cream
Ham
Lamb
Milk
Rabbit
Refined sugar
Veal

Shopping List

Tins and packets – 100 g (4 oz) quantities unless otherwise stated

	Kcals	kJ
Meat and meat products		
Stewed steak with gravy	176	730
Corned beef	217	905
Beef steak pudding	223	934
Beef stew	119	498
Bolognese sauce – 10½ oz (298 g) can	381	1593
Cannelloni	285	1191
Beef curry	136	568
Haggis	193	807
Beef meatballs in tomato sauce	163	681
Chicken stew	87	365
Beefburgers	251	1051
Liver pâté	408	1705
Chunky chicken	176	735
Minced beef and onions	164	686
Skinless beef sausages – 12 oz (340 g)	1320	5517
Sliceable chicken breasts	255	1065
Fish		
Fish paste	169	704
Herrings in tomato sauce – 7 oz (198 g) can	305	1275
Snacks and soups		
Ravioli	104	438
Spaghetti rings with tomato sauce	69	289
Baked beans	100	418
Spanish rice	103	432
Ready to serve cream of chicken soup 14¾ oz (418 g) can	280	1170
Ready to serve cream of tomato soup 10½ oz (298 g) can	220	920
Ready to serve vegetable soup 10¼ oz (291 g) can	113	472
Sauces and stuffings		
Chilli sauce – 1 fl oz (25 ml)	12	50
Cranberry sauce – 15 ml (1 tbsp)	65	272
Horseradish sauce – 15 ml (1 tbsp)	12	50

	Kcals	kJ
Bread sauce – 15 ml (1 tbsp)	32	134
Piccalilli – 15 ml (1 tbsp)	24	100
Barbecue cook-in-sauce – 13¼ oz (376 g) can	325	1358
Sweet and sour cook-in-sauce – 13¼ oz (376 g) can	233	974
Sage and onion stuffing	404	1688
Desserts		
Banana desserts	94	392
Butterscotch desserts	113	475
Strawberry desserts	96	402
Black cherry sponge pudding	316	1324
Chocolate sponge pudding	345	1442
Sultana sponge pudding	356	1488
Chocolate blancmange powder	520	2173
Custard powder	118	496
Cakes and biscuits		
Sponge cake mix	496	2073
Cream crackers	440	1857
Crispbread, rye	321	1367
Crispbread, wheat, starch reduced	388	1642
Gingernuts – per biscuit	51	213
Shortbread – per biscuit	64	268
Fruit cake, rich	332	1403
Madeira cake	393	1652
Jam sponge cake	302	1280
Miscellaneous		
Coca-cola	39	168
Lemonade	21	90
Ribena, undiluted – 1 fl oz (25 ml)	83	347
Milk shake syrup, fruit flavour – 1 fl oz (25 ml)	35	146
Country Store – 25 g (1 oz)	105	439
Rice Crispies – 25 g (1 oz)	100	418
Stuffed olives	52	217

Index

Note: Figures in italics indicate illustrations

Alcoholic drinks (*table*) 117
  calorie content (*table*) 119
Almond:
  and blackberry meringue 52, *52*
  lace wafers 103
  with chicken and ham 48
Anchovy and beef roulades 75
Angina 9
Animal fats 12. *See also* Fats,
  saturated
Apple:
  and grapefruit whip 98
  and loganberry walnut crumble
    97
  and orange liqueur fool 36
  baked mango and honey apples
    96, *96*
  chicken and apple salad 27
  poached in cider 95
  with soused cod 71
Applenut spice squares 103
Apricot:
  and ginger whip 27
  meringue basket 43
  stuffed lamb *44*, 45
  water ice 95
Artichokes: cod cutlets with
  Jerusalem artichoke sauce 71
Atherosclerosis 9
  adolescent beginnings, dietary
    prevention 16
  age factor 10
  improvement of, by diet 15
Aubergine:
  hors d'oeuvre 61
  spiced 86
  stuffed 74, *74*
  with spiced veal 78
Autumn pudding *22, 23*
Avial (Aviyal) 41
Avocado:
  and grapefruit salad 37
  and tomato rice salad 92

Bacon:
  and cottage cheese flan 28
  stuffed turkey 51
Balance, in planning low-cholesterol
  meals 20
Bamboo shoots with veal 49
Bananas in honey orange sauce 25,
  25
Baps, herby pizza 107
Barbeque sauce 115
  spicy 37
Bean sprouts with fried rice and
  mushrooms 49

Beans:
  chilli bean salad 38
  green beans and mushrooms in
    wine 86, *87*
Beef 14, 17
  and anchovy roulades 75
  and lamb, kebabs 37
  and mushroom loaf 72
  and tomato soup 48
  beefy onion soup 58
  crispy cottage pie 74
  in vermouth marinade 75, *75*
  minced, with peppers 22
  moussaka 73
  mustardy braised sirloin 73
  pasta-topped Italian beef
    casserole 72
  potted 51
  stuffed aubergines 74, *74*
  tarragon steaks with mushrooms
    35, *35*
  toad-in-the-hole 24, *24*
Beer, lamb chops braised in 78
Beetroot salad with walnut dressing
  90, *90*
Biscuits, dietary reduction 14, 17
Blackberry:
  and almond meringue 52, *52*
  shortcake 96
Blackcurrant:
  crunchy blackcurrant sundae
    26
  sorbet 95, *95*
Blood clotting mechanism, role of
  polyunsaturated fats 14
Blood pressure, high (hypertension),
  as risk factor 10, 11
Bread:
  garlic 111
  prune 103
  sauce 115
  soda 101
  spicy bread pudding 98
  wholemeal 101
Breakfasts 21
Broccoli, sesame 32
Buns:
  chocolate and orange 101
  nutty 105
Burgundy peaches 34
Butter 14, 17
Butterscotch:
  bars 55
  peaches, baked 99

Cabbage leaves, chicken stuffed
  109, *109*

Cake(s):
  chocolate orange 104
  dietary reduction 14, 17
  orange and sultana fruit loaf 102
  with Flora margarine 19
Calories:
  content of commonly used foods
    (*table*) 119–122
  fat, proportion of normal diet
    16
  in the cholesterol-lowering diet
    18, 19
Caper sauce 114
Caramel fruit condé 27
Carbohydrate reduction, in
  cholesterol-reducing diet 19
Carrot:
  and celery julienne 36
  and onion soup 60
  and parsnip croquettes 88, *88*
  chilli 87
Casseroles 21, 30
  chicken and pineapple 83
  lamb, in red wine 80, *80*
  Muscadet plaice 69
  mustardy chicken 81
  pasta-topped Italian beef 72
  sweet and sour rabbit 85
  turkey and grapefruit 83
Cauliflower:
  cheesy cauliflower provençale 87
  coriander 87
  soup 58
Celery:
  and carrot julienne 36
  braised, with cheese 107
  creamed, with baked potato 108
  sauce, stuffed cod cutlets with 68
Cereals:
  breakfast 21
  calorie content (*table*) 119
  cholesterol content (*table*) 117
  saturated fat content (*table*) 117
Cheese 14, 17
  and Marmite straws 54
  cauliflower provençale 87
  cheesy veal escalopes with
    noodles 34
  cottage 14
    and bacon flan 28
    home-made 116
  freely allowed 18
  sauce 114
  with braised celery 107
  stuffed tomatoes 89
Cheesecake, strawberry, quick 96
Chequerboard sandwiches 53

Chicken 14
   and apple salad 27
   and leek rissoles 80
   and pepper risotto 82
   and pineapple casserole 83
   and sweetcorn flan 82
   crunchy chicken salad 81
   garlic chicken with lemon
      sauce 82
   honey glazed 25
   in plum sauce 84, *84*
   lasagne 106
   melon bowl 61
   mustardy casserole 81
   piquant 110
   soup, farmhouse 58
   spicy boned 81
   -stuffed cabbage leaves 109, *109*
   Tandoori 39
   with ham and almonds 48
Children, cholesterol-lowering diet
   for 16
Chilli:
   bean, salad 38
   carrots 87
Chinese fruit salad 50
Chinese leaves, stir-fried, with
   orange 49
Chive dressings 114
Chocolate:
   and orange buns 101
   orange cake 104
   and orange mousse 98, *98*
   hazelnut creams 53
Cholesterol 12
   definition 10
   dietary, national differences 13
   food contents 14, (*table*) 117
   link with coronary heart
      disease 12
   -lowering diet. *See under* Diet
   rating system, for recipes 18, 20
   rich sources, avoidance of 17
   stepwise relationship with
      coronary heart disease 12
Choux puffs, savoury 54
Chowder, fish 60
Cider:
   and plaice bake 65
   apples poached in 95
   sauce, veal escalopes in 47
Cigar (cigarette) smoking. *See*
   Smoking
Cod:
   cutlets, with Jerusalem artichoke
      sauce 71
   savoury and cod bake 63
   smoked cod salad 31
   soused, with apple 71
   stuffed cutlets with celery sauce
      68
Coffee:
   fluff with mandarin oranges 33

Coffee (*contd*)
   froth delight 97
   semolina mousse 44
Colour, in serving 30
Condé, caramel fruit 27
Constitutional risk factors in
   coronary heart disease 10
Cooking fat 14, 17
Cooking ingredients
   calorie content (*table*) 121
   cholesterol and saturated fat
      content (*table*) 118
Cooking techniques 20
Cooking with polyunsaturates 19
Corn oil 14
Corn salad, lemon dressed 91
Coronary heart disease:
   children at risk, dietary advice for
      16
   constitutional risk factors 10
   definition 9
   environmental risk factors 10
   general dietary rules 16
   high risk groups, dietary rules 15
   link with cholesterol 12
   mortality, slowing down of
      rate 15
   risk factors 9, 10
Coronary thrombosis 9
Cottage pie, crispy 74
Courgettes:
   and mushroom salad 52
   au gratin 61
   in tomato sauce 34
   portugaise 88
   tuna stuffed 106
Cream 14, 17
Crumble, loganberry and apple
   walnut 97
Cucumber:
   and green pepper salad 90
   raita 40
Curried mushroom salad 45

Dairy products 17
   allowed freely 18
   calorie content (*table*) 120
   cholesterol content (*table*) 118
   dietary reduction 14
   saturated fat content (*table*) 118
   substitutes 116
Date crunchies 102
Devilled mushrooms 47
Diet:
   change in, effect on cholesterol
      levels 13
   cholesterol-lowering 14
   effectiveness 15
Drinks:
   calorie content (*table*) 119
   cholesterol, saturated fat content
      (*table*) 117
Dripping 14, 17

Dutch haddock flan 68

Eating out 30
Eggs 14, 17
   breakfast 21
   calorie content (*table*) 119
   cholesterol content (*table*) 117
   saturated fat content (*table*) 117
Entertaining 30
Environmental risk factors in
   coronary heart disease 10
Escalopes. *See under* Veal
Exercise, value of regularity 11

Fats:
   animal (saturated), dietary
      reduction 14
   calorie content (*table*) 119
   calorie percentage, of normal diet
      16
   cholesterol content (*table*) 117
   dairy, dietary reduction 14
   dietary, changes in, effects 13
   polyunsaturated
      as additive, effects 13
      cooking with 19
      dietary increase 14
         official recommendations 16
      effect on blood clotting
         mechanism 14
      reducing effects on cholesterol
         13
      role 13
   saturated
      food contents (*table*) 117
      how to cut down 17
   vegetable 12, 14
      in cooking 19
Fennel: chilled fennel salad 89
Fibre:
   content of foods (*table*) 122
   dietary, protective role 11
Fillings for sandwiches 54
Finland:
   coronary deaths compared with
      those of Japan 12
   dietary cholesterol 13
Fish 14. *See also under specific name*
   of fish
   allowed freely 18
   brick 18
      halibut baked in 69, *69*
   calorie content (*table*) 119
   cholesterol content (*table*) 117
   chowder 60
   Eastern spiced fish with rice 63
   fisherman's pie 65
   kebabs, marinated 64
   mushroom stuffed fillets 66
   saturated fat content (*table*) 117
   savoury tricorns 70
   seafood cocktail 62
   smoked cod salad 31

Fish (*contd*)
  spicy fish stuffed tomatoes 70
  white 18
Flan:
  chicken and sweetcorn 82
  cottage cheese and bacon 28
  Dutch haddock 68
  orange yogurt 94
  Provençale 61
  spiced meringue 46, *46*
Flapjacks, orange 104, *104*
Flavour 30
Flora margarine
  as savoury dressing 30
  at breakfast 21
  in cooking 19
Fool, plum 45
French dressing 113
Fruit 18, 20
  breakfast 21
  calorie content (*table*) 120
  cholesterol content (*table*) 117
  fresh fruit and yogurt salad 28
  fresh fruit kebabs 38
  salad, Chinese 50
  saturated fat content (*table*) 117
  spicy hot fruit salad 29
frying 19, 20

Garlic:
  bread 111
  chicken and lemon sauce 82
  golden garlic creamed
    potatoes 88
Ginger:
  and apricot whip 27
  lemon sauce, lamb chops in 79
  yogurt sauce with turkey 83
Grapefruit:
  and apple whip 98
  and avocado salad 37
  and mint cups 50
  and turkey casserole 83
Gravy 19, 115
Green beans and mushrooms in wine
  86, *87*

Haddock:
  Dutch haddock flan 68
  golden haddock soufflé 67, *67*
  paprika 65
  smoked, with stuffed peppers 108
Halibut baked in a fish brick 69,
  69
Ham with chicken and almonds 48
Hazelnut chocolate creams 53
Heart attack 9
Herby:
  pizza baps 107
  potatoes 89
  tomato sauce 113
Herrings with spinach 68
Hollandaise sauce, quick 114

Honey
  glazed chicken 25
  orange sauce, bananas in 25, *25*
Hors d'oeuvre, aubergine 61

Ice cream 17
Inherited disease associated with
  high cholesterol 12

Japan:
  coronary deaths compared with
    those of Finland 12
  dietary cholesterol 13
Jelly, melon and wine 32

Kebabs:
  beef and lamb 37
  fish, marinated 64
  fresh fruit 38
  Seekh 39
Kedgeree, kipper 111
Kitchri 40

Lamb 14, 17
  and lentils and carrots 80
  apricot stuffed 44, 45
  beef and lamb kebabs 37
  casseroled in red wine 80, *80*
  chops, braised in beer 78
    in lemon ginger sauce 79
  marinated, with orange mint
    sauce 79
  sherried chump chops with
    mushrooms 79
  Somerset lamb and vegetable
    layer 23
Lard 14
Lasagne, chicken 106
Leek:
  and chicken rissoles 80
  and mushroom salad 90
  chilled, in red wine 35
  in yogurt sauce 107
  soup, Bavarian 60
Lemon:
  chive dressing 114
  dressed corn salad 91
  ginger sauce, lamb chops in 79
  liqueur water ice 41, *41*
  mushroom and lemon soup 33
  tart, glazed 94, *94*
Lignin 12
Linoleic acid 14
Loganberry and apple walnut
  crumble 97

Mackerel, smoked
  and tomato salad 67
  paté 60
Mango and honey apples, baked 96,
  96
Margarine 17. *See also* Flora
  cooking 19

Margarine (*contd*)
  hard 14
Marinades 30
  vermouth, beef in 75, *75*
Marinated fish kebabs 64
Mayonnaise 17
  sunflower 113
Meat:
  allowed freely 18
  balls (veal) in tomato sauce 110,
    110
  calorie content (*table*) 120
  cholesterol content (*table*) 117
  fatty 17
  pasties, spicy 108
  saturated fat content (*table*) 117
Melon:
  and wine jelly 32
  chicken melon bowl 61
  fruit cups 93
Meringue flan, spiced 46, *46*
Milk:
  calorie content (*table*) 120
  cholesterol content (*table*) 118
  polyunsaturated filled 18, 116
  saturated fat content (*table*) 118
  skimmed 14, 18, 21
Minced meat, fat reduction 18
Mint and grapefruit cups 50
Moussaka, beef 73
Mousse:
  chocolate and orange 98, *98*
  coffee semolina 44
  salmon, with spring onion
    curls 66
Muffins, fluffy bran 101
Muscadet casseroled plaice 69, *69*
Mushrooms:
  a la greque 62
  and beef loaf 72
  and courgette salad 52
  and green beans in wine 86, *87*
  and leek salad 90
  and lemon soup 33
  and veal pie 77
  devilled 47
  fried rice with mushrooms and
    bean sprouts 49
  mushroom rice salad 38
  stuffed fish fillets 66
  veal and mushroom pancakes 26
  with sherried chump chops 79
Mustard sauce 114
Mustardy braised sirloin 73
Mustardy chicken casserole 81

Naans 40
Noodles: cheesy veal escalopes with
  noodles 34
Nuts:
  as garnishing 30
  calorie content (*table*) 121
Nutty buns 105

Nutty scones 103

Offal 14, 17
Onion:
  and carrot soup 60
  and tomato soup 59
  beefy onion soup 59
  salmon mousse with spring onion
    curls 66
  sauce 115
Orange:
  and chocolate mousse 98, *98*
  and sultana fruit loaf 102
  apple and orange liqueur fool 36
  bananas in honey orange sauce
    25, *25*
  chocolate and orange buns 101
  chocolate orange cake 104
  coffee fluff with mandarin oranges
    33
  flapjacks 104, *104*
  mint sauce, with marinated
    lamb 79
  South Sea oranges 93
  Victoria sandwich 102
  with stir-fried Chinese leaves 49
  yogurt flan 94
Overweight:
  as risk factor 11
  cholesterol-reducing diet for 18

Paella 108
Pancakes, veal and mushroom 26
Parsley:
  rice 36
  sauce 115
Parsnip and carrot croquettes 88,
  88
Pasta:
  and tomato salad 91
  Italian pasta salad 52
  savoury cod and pasta bake 63
  -topped Italian beef casserole 72
Pasties, with Flora margarine 19
Pastry 17
  shortcrust, all-in-one 100
  wholemeal, all-in-one 100
Paté, smoked mackerel 60
Pavlova, raspberry 97
Peach(es):
  and jelly, crisp 55
  Burgundy 34
  butterscotch, baked 99
Peanut butter cookies 105
Peanuts 19
Pectin 12
Peppers:
  and chicken, risotto 82
  green, and cucumber salad 90
  salad 51
  stuffed, with smoked
    haddock 108
  with minced beef 22

Personality, as risk factor 10, 11
Physical inactivity, as risk factor 11
Pilaf, brown rice 111
Pineapple:
  and chicken casserole 83
  tutti frutti pineapple rings 47
Pinwheel sandwiches 53
Pipe smoking. *See* Smoking
Pizza:
  baps, herby 107
  wholemeal 111
Plaice:
  and cider bake 65
  florentines 64
  Muscadet casseroled 69
Plant fibres, dietary, protective role
  11
Platelets, blood 14
Plum(s):
  Betty 93
  fool 45
  rosy plum ice 23
  sauce, chicken in, with courgettes
    84, *84*
Polyunsaturated fats. *See under* Fats
Pork 14, 17
Potato:
  baked, with creamy celery 108
  golden garlic creamed
    potatoes 88
  golden potato wedges 32
  herby 89
Potted beef 51
Poultry 18
  calorie content (*table*) 120
Poussins with sultana stuffing 42,
  43
Prawns 17
Preserves:
  calorie content (*table*) 121
  cholesterol content (*table*) 118
  saturated fat content (*table*) 118
Prostaglandins 14
Provençale flan 61
Prune bread 103

Quiche tartlets 54

Rabbit 18
  braised in sherry 84
  carbonade 85
  sweet and sour rabbit
    casserole 85
Raisin sauce, veal in 77
Raita, cucumber 40
Raspberry pavlova 97
Refined foods, as risk factor 11
Restaurant eating 31
Rhubarb, crispy baked 94
Rice:
  avocado and tomato rice salad 92
  brown rice pilaff 111
  fried, with mushroom and bean

Rice (*contd*)
  sprouts 49
  mushroom rice salad 38
  parsley 36
Risk factors. *See under* Coronary
  heart disease
Risotto:
  chicken and pepper 82
  veal and sweetcorn 28
Roasting of meat 19
Roe 17
Rosy plum ice 23
Roughage, dietary, protective
  role 11

Safflower oil 21
Salad:
  avocado and grapefruit 37
  avocado and tomato rice 92
  beetroot with walnut dressing 90,
    90
  chicken and apple 27
  chilled fennel 89
  chilli bean 38
  Chinese fruit 50
  Chinese vegetable 91
  courgette and mushroom 52
  crunchy chicken 81
  fresh fruit and yogurt 28
  Italian pasta 52
  leek and mushroom 90
  lemon dressed corn 91
  mushroom rice 38
  pasta and tomato 91
  pepper 51
    green, and cucumber 90
  smoked cod 31
  smoked mackerel and tomato 67
  spicy hot fruit 29
Salmon:
  gratiné 42
  mousse, with spring onion
    curls 66
Sandwiches:
  chequerboard 53
  fillings 54
  pinwheel 53
Sauces 17, 30
  all-in-one 114
  barbecue 115
  bread 115
  caper 114
  celery, with stuffed cod cutlets 68
  cheese 114
  cider, with veal escalopes 47
  coating 114
  ginger yogurt, with turkey 83
  herby tomato 113
  Hollandaise, quick 114
  honey orange, bananas in 25, *25*
  Jerusalem artichoke, with cod
    cutlets 71
  lemon, with garlic chicken 82

Sauces (*contd*)
    ginger, lamb chops in 79
    mustard 114
    onion 115
    orange mint, with marinated
        lamb 79
    parsley 115
    plum, chicken in 84, *84*
    raisin, veal in 77
    spicy barbecue 37
    tartare 115
    tuna, with spaghetti 112
    yogurt, leeks in 107
Savoury:
  choux pastry 54
  fish tricorns 70
Scones, nutty 103
Seafood cocktail 62
Sedentary work, as risk factor 11
Seekh kebabs 39
Semolina: coffee semolina
    mousse 44
Sesame broccoli 32
Seventh Day Adventists, coronary
    heart disease mortality 13
Shellfish 17
Sherry:
  rabbit braised in 84
  veal braised in 32
Shortcake, blackberry 96
Shrimps 17
Slimming 16, 18, 20
Smoked:
  cod, salad 31
  mackerel, paté 60
Smoking, as risk factor 10, 11
Somerset lamb and vegetable layer
    23
Sorbet, blackcurrant 95, *95*
Soufflé, golden haddock 67, *67*
Soups 17
  beef and tomato 48
  beefy onion 58
  carrot and onion 60
  cauliflower 58
  farmhouse chicken 58
  hearty winter broth 59
  leek, Bavarian 60
  mushroom and lemon 33
  thick vegetable 37
  tomato and onion 59
South Sea oranges 93
Soya bean oil 14, 21
Spaghetti with tuna sauce 112
Spiced (spicy):
  barbecue sauce 37

Spiced (spicy) (*contd*)
  boned chicken 81
  bread pudding 98
  fish stuffed tomatoes 70
  hot fruit salad 29
  meat pasties 108
  meringue flan 46, *46*
  veal with aubergines 78
Spinach, with herrings 65
Stews 21
Stock 30
Strawberry cheesecake, quick 96
Stress, as risk factor 10, 11
Stuffings 30
Suet 14, 17
Sultanas:
  orange and sultana fruit loaf
    102
  poussins with sultana stuffing 42
    43
Sundae, crunchy blackcurrant 26
Sunflower mayonnaise 113
Sunflower seed oil 14
Sweet and sour rabbit casserole 85
Sweetcorn:
  and chicken flan 82
  and veal risotto 28

Tandoori chicken 39
Taramasalata 17
Tarragon steaks with mushrooms
    35, *35*
Tartare sauce 115
Tarts and tartlets
  glazed lemon 94, *94*
  quiche 54
  tunafish 112
Texture 30
Toad in the hole, beef 24, *24*
Tomato(es):
  and beef soup 48
  and onion soup 59
  and pasta salad 91
  and smoked mackerel salad 67
  cheesy stuffed 89
  sauce, herby 113
  spicy fish stuffed tomatoes 70
Trace metals, dietary, as risk factor
    11
Tunafish:
  sauce, with spaghetti 112
  stuffed courgettes 106
  tartlets 112
Turkey:
  bacon stuffed 51
  grapefruit casserole 83

Turkey (*contd*)
  with ginger yogurt sauce 83
Tutti frutti pineapple rings 47

Veal 14, 18
  and mushroom pancakes 26
  and mushroom pie 77
  and mustard olives 76, 77
  and sweetcorn risotto 28
  braised in sherry 32
  escalopes, cheesy, with noodles 34
  escalopes in cider sauce 47
  escalopes in wine 77
  in raisin sauce 77
  meatballs in tomato sauce 110,
    110
  spiced with aubergines 78
  tagliatelle 76
  with bamboo shoots 49
Vegetable fats. *See* Fats, vegetable
Vegetables 18, 20
  as garnishing 30
  calorie content (*table*) 121–122
  cholesterol content (*table*) 118
  crispy stir-fried 89
  puréed 30
  saturated fat content (*table*) 118
  thick vegetable soup 37
Vegetarians, coronary heart disease
    mortality 13
Vermouth marinade, beef in 75, *75*
Victoria sandwich, orange 102

Wafers, almond lace 103
Walnut:
  dressing with beetroot salad
    90, *90*
  loganberry and apple walnut
    crumble 97
Water ice:
  apricot 95
  lemon liqueur 41, *41*
Weight reduction. *See* Slimming
Wine:
  chilled leeks in red wine 35
  lamb casserole in red wine 80, *80*
  melon and wine jelly 32
  veal escalopes in wine 77

Yogurt:
  fresh fruit and yogurt salad 28
  in sauces 30
  low-fat 14, 18
    home-made 116
  orange yogurt flan 94
  sauce, leeks in 107